TEE BALL MYTHS & SOLUTIONS

Developing a lifetime love for baseball

By Marty Schupak
First Edition

Table of Contents

TEE BALL MYTHS & SOLUTIONS

Marty Schupak
9 Florence Court
Valley Cottage, NY 10989

To order copies, call 845-536-4278.

Chapter 1

Introduction

Father 1: *What's the score?*
Mom: *They don't keep score in tee ball. They play for fun.*
Father 2: *Our team has had 13 fun times. The other team has had 5 fun times.*

If this is your first step into the world of tee ball—or even your third season—you'll walk away from this book a better coach. That, I guarantee. You might not agree with every word. Good. Think, challenge, invent. Carve your own coaching path. Even parents—those joyful, restless souls eager to take their child to the backyard with a ball and bat—will find something here. If you love the game and your child, you're already halfway there.

Depending on the source, over a million kids play tee ball each year. Every spring, SUVs and coffee cups head to ballfields, dreams in tow. Some parents want to spark a lifelong love for baseball. Others just want an hour's quiet. Some stare into phones while coaches try to teach another parent's child how to hold a glove. And yet, beneath the chaos, the goal is noble: teach kids to hit, throw, run, and laugh. The problem? Expectations. They tend to bloom faster than reality can follow. I know—I've been there. I was a father who wanted his kids to know the game before they even knew their letters. I had visions of home runs at age five. I was, of course, completely and utterly wrong.

I've been lucky. My life wandered into youth sports like a river finding its bend. I earned a Master's Degree in Physical Education from Arizona State, and while I never taught in an elementary school, perhaps I should have. Coaching my kids was the spark; writing about it was the fire. For those of you new to this journey, I say this: you are richer than you think. These years vanish. One moment they're learning to swing, and the next they're walking down the aisle. I've lived through joy, frustration, suspensions, friendships, feuds, championships, heartbreaks—all from the dugout. And I wouldn't change a second of it.

Now, back to tee ball. I've spent 30 years in youth sports and the last decade buried in tee ball. I began as a league commissioner, then authored two books: *T-Ball Skills & Drills* and *T-Ball Drills*. My video of the same title did well on Amazon, and on YouTube, it's topped 200,000 views. Am I the world's foremost authority? Probably not. But I've seen what works—and more importantly, what doesn't. I've seen kids drift away from baseball to soccer and lacrosse, not because they love those more, but because we failed to keep them engaged. That's what I aim to fix.

You'll find references to my other work sprinkled throughout this book. I'm not here to sell, but to share. Resources will be listed at the end—most free. You'll also hear stories. Not because I enjoy hearing myself talk, but because mistakes—mine and others'—are your best teachers. If I wander into a tale from 30 years ago mid-drill, trust that it's there for a reason.

I begin with ten myths that plague tee ball. I challenge them and offer solutions—take them, build on them, or reject them, but always keep the kids in mind. You'll also find drills, tested and true, drawn from my earlier books and field-tested over countless practices.

Above all, know this: I've written this not to bury tee ball, but to raise it up—to make it better, smarter, and more joyful for every child who steps to the tee.

Play ball.

Chapter 2

Myth #1: All Kids Learn Baseball Skills In Tee Ball

Years ago, I remember watching a tee ball coach divide his team in half for the first activity at his first practice. He gave one side a ball and told the players to have a catch. This was before soft-covered baseballs were plentiful, so it is not entirely the coach's fault. But what happened was two of the kids were hit in the face with a hard ball. Needless to say, neither of those kids stepped on the field ever again to play baseball or softball. And who knows, maybe one of them could have ended up being a star for their high school baseball or softball team. Remember, when you get your tee ball team on the field, don't assume anything about the skill of each player. This is a general rule of thumb. Maybe you coached some of the kids in soccer that Fall or knew their older brother or sister who were great athletes, but in general, if you are meeting a player for the first time, make sure you take baby steps.

When parents decide to become tee ball coaches, they probably have had some background in athletics. Maybe they played baseball or softball as a kid growing up or played on their varsity high school team. Whatever the case, most parents who coach come into the season with high expectations, and they expect the kids on their team to learn most of the baseball skills in a three or four-month period. This is tee ball myth #1. Most kids who are 5 or 6 years-old will be at the same or just slightly better baseball skill level than they were at the start of the season when the season ends. Of course, like I said, there are some kids who 1) are returning from the previous year, and 2) there are some exceptional athletes. Also, keep in mind that kids who have older brothers or sisters, who are very good athletes, will tend to be ahead of the other kids. Am I saying you won't see any real noticeable progression from the kids on your team? No, what I am saying is that we tend to have much higher expectations than reality. Also, keep in mind that kids will develop differently. I have seen 5 year-olds more physically developed than some 6 year-old kids, which is usually not the norm. I don't want to burst your bubble or take the air out of your enthusiasm if you couldn't wait to coach your son or daughter. I'm not saying the whole tee ball season is a waste. It's not, and we need good coaches like yourself or your neighbor. But you must have realistic expectations of what you are going to accomplish during the 10 or 12 weeks your team is together. I will get into individual skills later, but take throwing, for instance. A five-year-old kid will not show much improvement with any throwing technique throughout a tee ball season.

Tee ball coaches and parents can and will get frustrated with some kids when it is no one's fault. Many times, the coach will instruct a player how to do something, and the players won't get it. Why does this happen? It's a combination of their physical ability and their ability to take instructions. Some kids just cannot absorb or understand the instruction, or physically cannot do the task. For example, when I teach throwing to tee ball players, I emphasize keeping their head steady by focusing on a target they probably won't come close to and bringing their arm all the way back. I've had many players who did not bring their arm back, though they thought they did. What I did was create a drill called the "Bench Throwing Drill." I took a free-standing bench and had the player lie down on it. I stood at the foot of the bench and had them bring their arm all the way back and toss me the ball. The gravity helped bring their arm all the way back so they felt what it was like for the first time.

Sometimes, as the saying goes, there is more than one way to skin a cat. For the moment, let's both agree that it's hard to teach

12 kids who are 5 or 6 to improve their baseball skills in the course of 10 or 12 weeks. Do we just ditch the season and have kids get together and have snacks? No way! The tee ball season can and should be a positive experience with one goal in mind. To get kids to sign up for the next year, with the long-term goal of having the kids develop a lifetime love for baseball or softball. So, what is the solution for the tee ball myth that all kids learn baseball skills in tee ball?

Solution of Tee Ball Myth #1

For this myth, I think the solution lies in how we approach the entire season. Leagues, tee ball commissioners, parents, and coaches should see the coach's role as part tee ball instructor and part physical education teacher. The exact balance may vary—maybe 50/50, maybe even 75/25 leaning toward PE teacher—but what matters is that this mindset gives players a far better chance of staying engaged and excited.

The question now comes into how we carry out this plan for the season? You can take any approach you want, but I can tell you that in my 30 years of coaching youth sports, my first 10 years were a lot of trial and error, and the information I'm sharing with you is a positive approach, but you have to run the team as best you see it. As a coach, my expertise was in drills and running efficient practices. I coached from tee ball up to high school in multiple sports. My practices were very popular, and I developed my own formula where I'd do 2 or 3 skill drills, then run a fun game. I created drills over the years and began to log them. I was asked by my league to run a clinic on how to run an efficient, stimulating practice. Some good things were said about me, and I began doing these clinics around the country with some excellent feedback. The one thing I learned over the years was to be flexible and ABL (Always Be Learning). Some of the best drills I've picked up came not just from other coaches, but even from players who'd say, "Coach, what if we try it this way?" No matter the sport—tee ball, soccer, anything—you've got to mix in fun drills or games. Think it doesn't work? Let me share a story.

I'm a huge NFL fan and in the summers I like to watch different teams' practices. One sweltering day, the temperature was over 100 degrees. The players had already been grinding in full pads for two and a half hours, and they were clearly spent. Then, at the very end of practice, a Hall of Fame coach set up a quick game of touch football between the offensive and defensive linemen. The twist? Whichever group lost, their position coaches would have to run a lap in the brutal heat. Suddenly, these exhausted players lit up —laughing, shouting, competing like kids again. When the defensive coaches lost and had to run, the players roared with energy, cheering them on like it was the highlight of the day. In an instant, a team that looked completely drained was fully alive again. If a silly little game can recharge professional athletes in their 20s and 30s, imagine what it can do for 12-year-olds—or even tee ball players. Fun works at every level, as long as the coach uses it wisely.

In tee ball, the goal is to spark a love for baseball or softball. That's why the season should blend skill-building with fun, familiar activities—especially early on. The trick is to take games kids already know and give them a baseball twist. For example, think about a classic relay race. Normally, two or more teams line up, and on "go," the first runner sprints around a cone, comes back, and tags the next teammate. Simple and familiar. Now, let's add a baseball element: each player runs with a glove on, carrying a ball inside it. To keep the ball from popping out, they have to squeeze their glove or secure it with their other hand. When they return, they pass the ball to the next runner, who repeats the process. It's still a relay race—easy to understand and fun to play—

but now it also reinforces a baseball skill. That's the kind of small adjustment that makes a big impact while keeping kids engaged.

There are plenty of classic kids' games that coaches can easily adapt with a baseball theme. A few examples include Red Light, Green Light, Kick the Can, Tag, Freeze Tag, Duck, Duck, Goose, and Simon Says. In each of these, simply having players wear their gloves—and adding a ball when it makes sense—instantly brings the game into the world of baseball while keeping it fun and familiar.

Your tee ball practices shouldn't be taken over by 100% games. We do want to get to some skills, but I want to emphasize, please try to approach the season this way: expose your kids to the skills of the game rather than being intent on having them excel at that particular skill. When you have realistic expectations, you will have realistic results. One last suggestion. If you are coaching tee ball, I'd expect this to be the start of a nice, long youth coaching career for most of you. New coaches tend to copy the way one of their own coaches did it back when. I tell all new coaches to try and develop their own philosophy. Taking inspiration from others is fine, but flexibility, creativity, and adaptability are essential for a long and fulfilling youth sports coaching career.

Chapter Review

1. Have realistic goals for the tee ball season. Expose kids to the sport, have them interact, and make friends.
2. Kids develop physically and emotionally at different paces.
3. Approach tee ball like you are a combination of a physical education teacher and tee ball coach.
4. A good approach to tee ball and coaching youth sports is to do 2 or 3 skill drills followed by a fun activity.
5. Perform kids games that players are familiar with and add a baseball theme to it.

Coaching Tip

Shorter practices in youth sports create an environment that is safer, more fun, and more effective for learning. They support skill development while honoring kids' natural energy levels and keeping the experience enjoyable and sustainable—for players, coaches, and families alike. In a 45-minute tee ball practice, it's better to have 6 short drills rather than 3 long ones.

Myth #2: Longer Practices Get More Done

I received my Master's Degree from Arizona State University in physical education. One of my professors, Dr. Richardson, said something that has stuck with me forever. "Never confuse activity with accomplishment." The point being that many people keep themselves busy but don't really accomplish a lot. This is true in a lot of different fields that have nothing to do with sports. I remember hearing the story of a famous Wall Street guy who was investigating a company he wanted to buy. He was escorted to their beautiful office building in Manhattan, and with his legal pad, he made notes as he went from floor to floor. He had a great reputation as an investor, but when he reviewed his notes, he was confused. He finally went out to their plant in the Midwest and spoke to the guy in charge out there. He told him very succinctly, "Joe, I can't figure out what those people do in the office all day in New York." Joe smiled and said," They do nothing. I'd get rid of every one of them." And that's exactly what he did. Sad but true, there are a lot of people who get paid a lot of money and don't produce a lot.

I observed one of his practices when my oldest son began playing baseball. It consisted basically of two hours of batting practice combined with some pitchers throwing on the sidelines. While watching, I saw how quickly the coach lost the team. More rocks were being thrown by the players in the field than baseballs.

That first season was a struggle, and after speaking to a member of the Board, I was told that if I thought I could do a better job, coach a team. So I threw my hat in the ring, got a team, and when I ran my first practice, it wasn't much better than the practices I had watched that first season. I realized there had to be a better way. After this questionable start in my youth coaching career, I decided to devote as much spare time as I had to researching and observing coaches at all levels and how they run their practices. I ran all over New York State and New Jersey, observing different sports practices with an emphasis on baseball. I covered almost all levels and even went up to West Point and watched their baseball team practice. The common elements I found in the most efficient practices were:

1. Every player was involved in every drill with little idle time.
2. The best practices I saw had the assistant coaches being utilized all the time.
3. Pep talks were limited; most communication focused on teaching, with feedback on what went right and what went wrong.
4. The transition between drills, going from one to another, was quick, with all the coaches running and displaying enthusiasm.
5. Fun drills were interspersed strategically to maintain engagement.
6. The practice started on time and ended on time, and on the youth level, it would end on a high note or with a fun drill.

On the youth level, ages 8-12, I would run practice for about 75 minutes, and sometimes it would only be an hour. This took effort with logging endless drills on my computer, then planning every practice on an index card with 5-7 drills and having one alternate drill in case one drill did not work that day. Planning a tee ball practice is simpler for the main reason that you are limited on what you want to accomplish. Obviously, going over the 6-4-3 double play is not the narrative you want to teach the players.

Practices in the local town's tee ball program are completely different from the practices at the University of Texas baseball team. But as coaches, we have to infuse the right formula to get the best results. Tee Ball practices do have an advantage over the upper levels of baseball and softball. You just don't need as much space. You will need ample space so you can spread your team out for safety's sake, but nothing like a diamond with 90' bases. You still must plan every practice. It is prudent for you to keep your practices shorter rather than longer. My recommendation from my experience with tee ball is to keep practices no longer than an hour. I would say that as the season goes on, trim the practices to 45-50 minutes.

One aspect of short practices is that there are parents who are going to be late for whatever reason. If a player misses 15 minutes of your practice because they're late, that's 25% of the practice they are missing. I found an easy workaround early on that I still recommend. As players arrive at practice, I assign each one a number—first to arrive is number one, second is number two, and so on. With older kids, I use these numbers to set the order for batting practice: number one bats first, number two bats second, and so forth. In tee ball, you can actually do the same thing. The order they arrive is the order they will bat at that practice. Another hint is at the Parents' Meeting to tell them this is how you determine the batting order for practice. And you can also do it this way for games. I learned at the beginning of my coaching career that team sports practices are competing with piano lessons, karate lessons, dance lessons, etc. When your practice gets to be so creative and stimulates all your players, you'll see something amazing. The parents will start to base extracurricular activities around your practices.

I do want to mention that nothing says your practices can't be longer than 60 minutes. If you have a special group of kids and they are good listeners and have enthusiasm for going longer, and you and your coaches have the stamina, by all means, practice longer. There are exceptions to everything.

When I coached 8 to12-year-olds, practices generally ran 60–75 minutes, which inspired the title of my first instructional video: The 59-Minute Baseball Practice. Instructions on accessing this resource for free are included in the resource section at the back of this book.

Solution of Tee Ball Myth #2

For this myth, my solution is to keep your practices no longer than 45-60 minutes for the majority of the season. With this, you must come up with a way to motivate parents to get their kids to practice on time. The number system, giving players a number as they arrive, works great! You can try any system you want, but the shorter practices will be more effective than longer practices. The longer the practices, the better the chance you will lose your kids emotionally, and you'll be in store for what I call "Wild Kingdom" where you lose control of the kids and they become wild. Before the season even begins, you should be developing your own list of drills. There are enough resources to get some great drills via the internet, your local library, the back of this book, and just speaking to coaches and parents involved in your local league.

When you structure your 45-minute practice, there will be some trial and error for you once the season begins. Over time, you will discover your rhythm, optimize transitions, and learn how best to utilize assistant coaches. Remember that it is better to do 6 drills for 8 minutes each than 4 drills for 12 minutes each. You shouldn't rush through each drill, so you may reduce the 6 drills to 5. You'll learn your own comfort zone as a coach and get a feel for working with your assistant coaches. The key is consistency, structure, and maintaining a positive, engaging environment for the players.

Chapter Review

1. Don't confuse activity with accomplishment. Have your practices planned in advance.

2. In general, longer practices often lead to decreased enthusiasm and engagement.

3. It is recommended that practices go from 45-60 minutes. You should get your own comfort zone with the length. Nothing is in concrete.

4. Develop your own list of drills before the season starts.

5. Don't be disappointed if your first couple of practices seem like duds. It is a work in progress.

Coaching Tip

Young athletes absorb skills through repetition and experience —not lectures. Begin each practice with a brief instructional talk. For example, say, "Let's meet at second base," and hustle there with the team. Rotate the starting base each practice, which helps players learn the layout of the field. Position yourself so that you face the sun while speaking, not the players; this prevents players from squinting and covering their eyes and keeps their focus on your instructions.

Myth #3: Parents' Meetings Aren't Needed

When I began my youth sports coaching career, I did not have a Parents' Meeting at the beginning of each season. I learned that it is necessary for the start of each season. Once I started doing this, parental complaints dropped around 50%, and the season seemed to run much smoother. When it comes to tee ball, a Parents' Meeting might seem unnecessary given the age and skill level of the players. I'd argue it's actually essential—and here's why. But before I get into the reasons, let me share two quick Parents' Meeting stories. When I used to do baseball coaching clinics nationwide, I had an interesting experience in Southern New Jersey. The clinic went very well, with a good showing of about 100-125 coaches and parents. My clinics usually last about 90 minutes with a break halfway through. The theme of the clinic was "How to Run a Baseball Practice." The clinic was about 70-80% on practice organization and drills. There was a portion on strategies that included 1st & 3rd offensive and defensive strategies, plus a lot of baserunning and bunting situational strategies. At every clinic, I always made sure to go over the importance of a Parents' Meeting and spent around 15 minutes talking about what to cover. At the clinic's conclusion, I handed out an evaluation paper, trying to get feedback so I could critique myself. After reading all of them, most of the comments were positive, except for one thing. About 25% of the attendees said, and I'm paraphrasing, that they could have done without the Parents' Meeting part of the clinic. And they preferred more strategies and drills. Now jump forward around 6 months. I received an email from one of the attendees. In it, part of what he said:

"I enjoyed your clinic a few months back. The one part I didn't take seriously enough was your part about a Parents' Meeting. What a mistake! I had several parents who were out of control. I realized that if I had gone over certain things before the season, there would have been a lot fewer problems. Never again! It was close, but I'm coaching again next year. I will surely have a Parents' Meeting. Thanks, coach!"

This is a perfect example of what could happen if you don't have a parents' meeting. Here is a coach who was skeptical, like me, when I first started coaching, and he had a difficult time.

On to story number two. In our local league, the team that wins the championship (for the age 11 & 12 year-old division) gets to coach the league All-Star team. This is a perk that coaches love. And in all years of coaching, I've never seen a coach pass on the opportunity to coach the All-Star team. This is the chance for the coach to have that player or players who, during the season, would say to themselves, "If only I had picked him for my team." It is a perk, but there is also added pressure that comes with it. This particular year, a friend and competitor of mine who coached another team became the All-Star coach. It was his first opportunity, and I was happy for him. Because I have been to this rodeo before, I approached him and suggested he have a Parents' Meeting before he begins practicing. He was cool to the advice, but being polite, asked me what he should go over. I gave him the intel, but he ended up never having the meeting. Running into him a few weeks later, he told me the experience was a disaster and that he should have had the Parents' Meeting. He even told me a couple of the worst parents were two from his own team. Okay, this book is about tee ball, but just a few thoughts for all of you who will go on to coach for more years and may end up coaching an All-Star team. Keep in mind that the players you are getting are the cream of the crop from your league. You have players who starred on their own team who played shortstop and maybe were the star pitcher. Now they are told they have to play in right field and bat ninth. This is hard for some kids to take and even harder for the parents. You must prepare the players and parents for this and other issues. When I coached All-Stars, my favorite speech would be to tell the group of 24 parents,

"If you are canceling a family summer trip to Cape Cod or to Europe, for this team, and can't accept your son playing right field and batting 9th or being on the bench, please reconsider his spot on this team. I'd rather you go away and have a good time. Besides, I have a couple of parents calling me every night trying to get their son on this team, and they are willing to sit on the bench."

Pretty strong but very effective. You will never experience anything as extreme as this in tee ball, but you can see the point I'm trying to make.

Solution of Tee Ball Myth #3

The solution for myth #3 that you don't need a Parents' Meeting in tee ball is to have one before the season begins. Here's the case for a Parents' Meeting in tee ball. I happen to think communication is one of the most important aspects of life. So much is lost in our world because of the lack of communication. The Parents' Meeting is the express lane where you establish not only who is in charge of the team but what the players and parents should expect in the upcoming tee ball season. I recommend the meeting to be no longer than 15-20 minutes.

Even though I try to keep the meeting low-key, I always organize it in such a way that the parents will know that I have put time into preparing for this meeting. I prepare a packet for each parent, and they sign a sheet of paper upon accepting the packet.

The packet will contain the agenda of the meeting, plus a page with the names of the coaches and their contact information, plus the names of the roster of players with their contact information. This is a good idea because many parents will carpool to and from practice.

Here is a list of things that might be on the agenda:

1. Introduction & background
2. Goal of the season (mention having fun)
3. Clothing
4. Importance of safety
5. Driving and parking in our facility
6. Limitations of skills to be learned
7. Practices, general time and place, and how many per week
8. Pick-ups and drop-offs for practice
9. Procedure for cancelling practices or games
10. Team Parent
11. Athletic progression varies with each child
12. Fan behavior during games
13. Equipment & water bottle
14. Game schedule
15. Team Newsletter
16. How we approach games
17. Volunteers for assistant coaches
18. Snack schedule

This list is not exhaustive—you can add or remove items as appropriate. The one thing I recommend is to keep it on your computer if you will continue to coach. As you move up into the different age groups, your Parents' Meetings will always be changing. As you get into the higher age groups where there is more competition, you will make a mental note during the season as problems arise, "I have to go over that next year before the season starts." Remember, you will never cut out all complaints. But you will be able to filter out a lot of them with a Parents' Meeting.

I just want to point out a few things from my list. Number three on my list is clothing. At my local field, early in the season, when the sun sets, the temperature at the beginning of the season can drop from the 60s to the 40s. Too many times, kids were cold in my dugout. So I made it a point that, early in the season, an extra top is advisable.

Number twelve mentions a water bottle. I tell parents I will be bringing a team jug of water, but I'd like to have each player bring their own water bottle with their name on it. Of course, there will be plenty of times when you are leaving the field, you'll find gloves, bats, and water bottles. Make sure you always have a permanent ink Sharpie in your car in case some items aren't labeled with a name.

Number nine is Team Parent. This is invaluable! Usually, I have the Team Parent before the meeting. The Team Parent will coordinate any change of practice or cancellation. I've never had a problem getting a team parent. I usually ask for a volunteer in my introductory letter a few months before the season begins. He or she is the conduit between the other parents and me.

Number thirteen is the team newsletter. At the meeting, I always ask for a volunteer to do a team newsletter, and I make it simple. It is one page and is put out three times during the season. After the first game, midway through the season, and after the last game. I only have two requirements: every player's name is mentioned with each newsletter, and it is not an email version but has to be a hard copy. The reason for this is so the parents can send a copy to the grandparents, who are retired and living in Florida, North Carolina, or Arizona. The grandparents love this and will bring the copy to their clubhouse or dining room to show off that their grandson hit a ball into the outfield and got a double. You, the coach, have got to see the final copy before it is handed out to the parents, so you can proofread it more for content than grammar. You will be feeding the person printing it the information, but you have to go over it.

Another important aspect of running a Parents' Meeting is that you, as a coach, will begin to get a reputation as an organized coach, and other parents will take notice. Plus, it is an excellent habit to get into. Remember that you will have a different mixture of parents on your team. You'll have single moms, parents who work two jobs, parents who are divorced, parents who don't give a darn about tee ball, and parents with other issues. Run your meeting like tee ball is a part of everyone's lives for the next three to four months. Also, there may be particular issues based on the facility your team plays. I mentioned above how cold our field got when the sun sets. If your league has certain rules, especially for safety, you can list those also.

For instance, I know that driving and parking at a facility with kids playing is always a safety issue. We had an instance once when someone ran into the bleachers with his car. It was an awful incident, and we had to put in certain safety parameters. And remember, just like kids will pick up a bat and start swinging, kids love to run and chase each other all over, so remind your parents to be aware.

I can't emphasize enough the importance of holding a Parents' Meeting as part of your coaching routine. Whether you're coaching tee ball or a 12U travel hockey team, it will make the season run much more smoothly. While it won't eliminate every complaint, it will certainly help prevent many of them.

Chapter Review

1.   Always hold a Parents' Meeting before the season starts. Even at the tee ball level, it sets the tone, reduces complaints, and makes the season run smoother.

2.   Come prepared with an agenda and parent packets. Include rosters, contact info, safety reminders, and basic expectations. A little organization goes a long way toward showing parents you've invested time in the team.

3.   Keep it short and focused. Fifteen to twenty minutes is usually plenty—respecting parents' time builds goodwill.

4.   Secure a Team Parent early. Having a reliable point of contact for cancellations, snack schedules, and updates makes your job as a coach much easier.

5.   Save and refine your notes each year. Coaching is a process. Keep your documents on file, add new lessons learned, and your Parents' Meetings will get stronger as you move up to older age groups.

Coaching Tip

When coaching a tee ball team, establishing a connection with the players is crucial. Speaking at their eye level, which can be achieved by kneeling, helps convey respect and builds a more trusting relationship. This approach allows players to feel heard and valued, making them more receptive to coaching instructions.

Myth #4: Tee Ball Coaches Must Be Experienced

Years ago, I was leaving work in a family business where I worked. My family had a third-generation Lumber & Building supply business, and our warehouse was in a rough area in the South Bronx. Coming home, I was driving North on 3rd Avenue heading to the Cross Bronx Expressway. If you've ever driven in any part of New York City, you know that going one mile can take forever between negotiating traffic and traffic lights. Stopped at a light, I peeked to my right and saw a woman with about six or seven kids throwing a ball to each one. I pulled over and politely approached the activity. When the right moment came, I approached a woman named Rosie. She was a single mom with two kids, working full-time, and she carried herself with a big presence. I asked if she ran some kind of after-school program, but she told me no—she had simply stepped up to be her son's tee ball coach because no one else wanted the job. When I asked about her experience, she laughed and admitted she had none. Aside from sitting on her father's lap to watch the Mets a few times, she knew nothing about baseball. Here was a working mother in a tough situation, with no background in the sport, yet she took on the responsibility of coaching a team. I only spoke with Rosie for about 15 minutes, but I left certain she would be a great coach. Why? One word: enthusiasm. In that short time, her energy and positivity poured out of her—and kids respond to that. So, can someone with no experience become a good tee ball coach? Absolutely. I'd take a "Rosie" with enthusiasm and leadership over a know-it-all ex–high school star any day. If tee ball is your first step into youth coaching, you can succeed as long as you have the desire. Yes, there will be a few bumps along the way, but there's plenty of guidance out there to help. Personally, I'd love to see more moms and dads step into coaching—whether as head coaches or assistants. The game, and more importantly the kids, will be better for it.

Solution of Tee Ball Myth #4

You do not need to have been a baseball or softball player to coach tee ball. What you do need is passion, patience, and the ability to show kids that you enjoy being out there with them. Remember that in tee ball, most of the kids will not excel at the baseball skills you're introducing to them. The goal is to expose kids to different skills while making sure they're having fun. For new coaches stepping into tee ball for the first time, here's an example from my own experience outside my comfort zone—it wasn't even baseball, it was soccer. Years ago, I became my daughter's soccer coach by default because her recreational league was short on coaches. What did I know about soccer? Absolutely nothing. My first step was to visit the local library and check out a few soccer books. Then I reached out to the local high school soccer coach I knew from baseball and asked if I could observe a few practices and maybe stand on the sidelines for a game. He welcomed me and even explained his decisions as he coached. I did the same with the women's varsity soccer coach and was able to observe a practice there as well. The point is simple: you have to be proactive when learning something new. My team wasn't very strong, but I made sure the kids had a positive, fun experience—and they did.

That same principle applies to tee ball. The point is, depending on the sport and level of play, don't be afraid to take on the job as a coach or even an assistant coach. If this were, let's say, a college-level Division 1 water polo team, there is no way I could ever consider trying to coach it with zero experience. But tee ball is something a parent with very little sports knowledge can handle. So again, the answer is yes, you can coach tee ball without any experience. At the end of this book, I have listed resources for first-year and experienced tee ball coaches.

One recommendation is to develop a master list of drills. If you take on your child's tee ball team in the fall for a spring season, use the months in between to research books and videos. Create a file on your computer titled "Tee Ball Drills"and list each drill with a brief explanation—just the name won't be enough to remember how it works months later. I've done this for every sport I've coached, and it's been incredibly helpful. The list is never final—you'll add new drills and retire others—but the best part is creating and naming your own drills.

And here's one more story that inspired me deeply. While researching this book, I came across Glenn Moscoso, who is confined to a wheelchair with cerebral palsy. Despite his disability, Glenn became his son's tee ball coach. His story is a reminder that if you're willing to step up, nothing should hold you back. Visit his website—wheelchairdaddy.com—and you'll see photos filled with smiles. It's not just about baseball; it's about what happens when parents invest in their kids.

Chapter Review

1. You need not have been on your high school baseball or softball team to coach tee ball.

2. The library and the internet have incredible resources that one can investigate and learn about tee ball.

3. Be proactive and speak to other experienced coaches and ask if you can observe a practice.

4. Develop a master list of tee ball drills once you are assigned to coach a team.

5. If you know you are going to want to eventually coach a tee ball team, throw your hat in to become an assistant coach for a year.

Coaching Tip

When coaching tee ball early in the season, separate skills at the first practice. If you are teaching catching, don't have the players throw the ball back to you. Just have them drop it to the side. If you are teaching throwing, don't have them catch the ball. Have them take the balls from a bucket. Separating skills early in the season helps kids learn better, build confidence without being overwhelmed, and enjoy the game more. It turns early-season practices into the building blocks for a fun, successful season of growth.

Myth #5: All 5–6 Year-Olds Develop Equally

Tee ball coaches need to know that kids progress physically and emotionally at a different pace. Years ago, I was the athletic director at a community center. I remember running a class called *Mommy & Me*, where we would do different games and physical activities with the mother and her child. During one activity, one mother started to cry uncontrollably in front of the whole class. I went up to her to calm her down. The reason for being upset was that she couldn't understand why her 4 year-old daughter could not do the same things as the others in the class. After I calmed her down, we continued the class. Afterward, I spoke to her, assuring her that kids are different. At the time, I was only a couple of years removed from graduate school for physical education, so my explanation involved some physiology and growth development on the most basic levels. She was fine for the rest of the classes.

That moment stuck with me because it perfectly captured a truth that every coach, especially a tee ball coach, needs to remember: comparison is natural, but it can also be damaging. Parents inevitably compare their kids to others. They want to know if their child is "keeping up." This mindset extends well beyond sports—it starts in preschool applications, continues in academic performance, and carries all the way through SAT scores, college admissions, and job opportunities. Youth sports, unfortunately, can become another arena for these comparisons. But if you, as the coach, understand the myth and address it, you can reduce much of the tension, frustration, and pressure that so often creeps into tee ball.

Let me quickly explain a few things about growth patterns. When a child is born, they go through speedy growth up to age five. A verified fact is that when the growth rate is rapid, learning new motor skills (their ability to move and coordinate their bodies) during this time is diminished. After five or when the child is in elementary school, this growth rate, which was speedy, begins to slow down. Believe it or not, this gives a window so that kids can learn motor skills. After this period, the speedy growth pattern takes over again until adolescence.[1]

What does this mean for the tee ball coach? If the points I've made are true—which I believe they are—then even between ages 5 and 6, you're likely to see noticeable differences in how children handle certain motor skills. Progression isn't determined by age alone. For example, a 5- or 6-year-old who plays with an older, athletic sibling may have already developed some basic athletic skills. It's not a guarantee, but in my experience, having an older athletic brother or sister often makes a visible difference on the tee ball field.

When parents start doing athletic activities at a young age, many times the parent expects more than is physically and anatomically possible. Should the enthusiastic parent not do an athletic activity with a 3 or 4 year-old? Absolutely not! The purpose of this writing is to deflect frustration from the parents, the coach, and even the player. There are always exceptions to everything. Years ago, I watched a father bring his young son onto The Mike Douglas Show. The boy, just two or three years old, was already hitting golf balls with remarkable accuracy. That child, of course, would grow up to become Tiger Woods—one of the greatest golfers of all time.

Even in high school, many factors beyond motor skills can influence athletic success. Take Michael Jordan, for example—he didn't make his high school varsity basketball team as a sophomore. At 5'11", the coach felt he lacked the skills and size for varsity and placed him on the junior varsity team instead. That setback, however, fueled his determination. He became the star of the JV team, grew four inches, and earned a spot on varsity as a junior.

Or consider David Robinson, another NBA great. When he entered the Naval Academy, he was tall—around 6'8"—but not yet the towering force he would become. During his freshman year, he hit a huge growth spurt, eventually reaching 7'1". That change transformed his game and set him on a path toward becoming one of the most dominant centers in basketball history.

The point of these stories isn't to compare your five year-old to professional athletes. It's to illustrate that growth and development are unpredictable. Greatness doesn't always appear early. Sometimes it takes years to emerge. And sometimes, what looks like a weakness—a smaller frame, a slower start—turns out to be the very trait that fuels resilience and determination later.

Solution of Tee Ball Myth #5

Hopefully, it's clear that kids progress at different rates, no matter what anyone tells you. As a tee ball coach, how can you address this myth?

First, bring it up at the Parents' Meeting. Explain to parents—backed by books and studies—that every child develops at their own pace. Acknowledge that it's natural for parents to compare their kids to teammates and sometimes feel a little envy if their child seems behind. You can share examples like Michael Jordan, David Robinson, or Jose Altuve—the Houston Astros star who, at 5'6", was considered too small to play professionally yet went on to an All-Star career and won the 2017 MVP.

Second, as a coach, make sure every player rotates through each position. In tee ball, the focus should be on giving every child the same number of repetitions. I remember when my middle son's coach only played certain kids in the infield, leaving others in the outfield. I spoke up and had my son moved to another team—

turns out several other parents felt the same way but were too intimidated to act. Fairness, in my view, should be non-negotiable at the tee ball level.

The third thing you can do is to be proactive when you think a parent on your team is bothered by something, either that you, the coach, did or something with their own child. Now this is tough to do. In my 30 years of coaching youth sports, I've seen some tough personalities. I've been yelled at, threatened, and had parents waiting for me at my house when I arrived home. But even though I was a shy kid growing up, I learnt that if you are proactive with problems in youth sports, you can solve the issue better, and the parent may not like you, but will respect you more. It can be any number of things that you notice, like a parent shaking their head at their child's lack of success. Or it can be the parent yelling loudly during the game or the practices. Maybe something got back to your assistant coach about how one of the parents is unhappy with the way his child is being handled. However you find out, and go with your instinct, you will be better off in the long run during the season and in your youth sports coaching career if you proactively approach the problem.

The fourth thing you can do takes some extra undertaking, but is effective. Handouts! I was a big believer in them. Now we don't want to inundate parents with reading material. But if you're a tee ball coach and are considering being involved in youth sports for the next 5-10 years, handouts are effective. Keep them short and to the point. For instance, if you were in the library and saw an article related to tee ball age kids, you may want to copy it and hand it out at the next practice. Here is an example:

Dear Parents,

While at the library, looking for creative ideas to enhance our tee ball season, I came across a passage from a book I'd like to share with you: If starting children early can create early burnout, why do parents feel pressured to force their child into a sports program? Some parents constantly compare their children to other children. They see other children participating and practicing sports skills in an organized setting. They worry that their children will be unable to catch up if they are not involved in a similar program. immediately. Although this is untrue, parents need reassurance, and they need facts...A key is to find programs that allow the child to participate regardless of ability...Children consider having fun and improving their skills to be much more important than winning. [2]

This really hits home a few points. But for you, the coach, handouts can be very effective. Don't overdue this. If you are playing a ten-game tee ball season, maybe 3-5 handouts are appropriate. There is no rule of thumb here, so you are on your own if you want to do the extra work.

The fifth thing you can do is organize drills by ability—but this requires a delicate touch. I'm a strong believer in using assistant coaches, and this is especially important in tee ball, where kids might randomly pick up bats and swing or throw balls like paper airplanes.

Since some players are returning from previous seasons, I like to use stations and different drills. Sometimes it helps to divide the team by ability for certain drills. However, be aware: kids notice if one group is doing something "advanced" that they aren't. They may feel left out or think the other group has better skills.

The key is balance—don't overdo it, but occasional ability-based drills can be effective. Kids are smart, often smarter than we realize, so handle these divisions thoughtfully. Done correctly, this approach can help everyone improve without causing frustration.

You'll be fine during the season if you make the parents aware of how kids progress differently. There are exceptions but for the most part, I've laid out the best way to approach the situation.

Chapter Review

1.   All kids progress at different paces—there is no one-size-fits-all.

2.   Some parents will be overly concerned when their child can't do what another is doing.

3.   Examples like Michael Jordan, David Robinson, and Jose Altuve remind us that greatness develops in many ways.

4.   Tee ball coaches should rotate players in the field and in the batting order.

5.   Be proactive if you sense a problem is brewing with a parent.

6.   In practice, once in a while, divide the team by ability and utilize assistant coaches in the different groups to run drills.

7.   Handouts are constructive if the topic is appropriate. Don't overdue it.

Coaching Tip

Learn every player's name as soon as possible. A child hearing their name from a coach makes them feel valued and respected. It fosters a sense of identity, belonging, and security, while also serving as a foundation for different skills. Dale Carnegie once said that a person's name is the sweetest sound to them. For a young child, it builds identity, confidence, and a sense of belonging. In tee ball, where kids are just beginning their sports journey, that simple act can make a difference.

Myth #6: Tee Ball Teams Don't Need Multiple Assistants

Some people step into tee ball coaching thinking their strong personality is enough, and that assistant coaches will just get in the way. If that's you, trust me: your practices will be more effective, your team will learn more, and you'll become a better coach if you know how to utilize assistants. Limiting the number of helpers might seem doable, but it comes with risks.

The biggest concern for everyone—league, parents, and players—is safety. Young tee ball players will naturally pick up bats lying around and swing them. You can never have too many eyes on the field. My family experienced a frightening accident that illustrates just how fast these things happen. Years ago, I was coaching 8- and 9-year-olds in a Little League® rookie division. During a hitting drill, my middle son bent down to pick up a ball as my assistant coach swung a bat. The bat struck my son's head, and he needed 27 stitches. He was fine, but it was a vivid lesson in how quickly accidents can occur. Even in tee ball, the more adults watching, the fewer the chances for serious injuries. And a side note: if you ever need emergency stitches like this, ask for the plastic surgeon on call—it can make a huge difference.

Assistant coaches aren't just for safety—they're essential for running a positive, engaging practice. At the Parents' Meeting, I tell all parents that I've listed them as assistant coaches. Some are shocked, even resistant, citing work or other commitments. I explain clearly: unless you're skipping practices and games entirely, I need and expect your help. A fair commitment is one practice and one game per set of parents. I reassure them that even if they know nothing about sports or baseball, they can focus on safety and helping kids enjoy the game. Plus, being involved can make them more creative and engaged parents overall.

The myth that tee ball teams don't need many assistants couldn't be further from the truth. Sure, you can coach with only one or two helpers in extreme situations—Rosie, the single mom from the South Bronx, did it. She had little experience, and likely minimal help, yet she persevered. Admirable? Absolutely. But wouldn't it have been better if she'd had several engaged parents around to share the load? The point is simple: assistant coaches aren't optional—they're vital.

Solution of Tee Ball Myth #6

As the head coach of a youth sports team, you have to be part teacher, part manager, and yes, part salesman. Part of your job as manager is to convince 24 adults—assuming 12 players on a tee ball team—that they are needed. You set the tone at the Parents' Meeting, starting with something like:

"The success of this tee ball team will depend not just on the coaches, but on the enthusiasm and commitment of every adult in this room."

Always use "we" when describing the goals of the team. Some parents will push back—many are single parents with busy schedules—but if they plan to attend games, they must help out in some way.

With multiple assistant coaches, you can divide the team into smaller groups, implement drills for different skill levels, and provide more individualized attention. More coaches also improve supervision, which is critical for safety with young players, and they create opportunities to learn and grow into future head coaches.

To ease initial concerns, explain to parents that you don't expect the kids to master all baseball skills in 3–4 months. The primary goal is exposure to baseball, ensuring the kids have fun and want to return next season. Limited knowledge of baseball is okay —the need for assistants is first and foremost safety. Assisting with drills and retrieving balls keeps practices flowing smoothly, and sharing even a small amount of time with the team pays dividends.

Some parents will inevitably break commitments, but that's part of managing the team. Your job is to maintain structure for the benefit of the kids.

Here's another reason assistant coaches are essential: the "residual effect." When a parent steps in—even just once—they can become more involved long-term. I've seen this firsthand. One year, I coached a 10–12-year-old team that lacked talent. Inspired by an NFL coach, I spent extra time on baserunning drills. The residual effect? Players paid closer attention on the field, improving overall performance.

The same principle applies to tee ball. I had a parent who was initially reluctant—limited athletic ability, demanding job—but he showed enthusiasm and commitment. After helping at practices, he went on to umpire league games and remained involved for years. A small spark of involvement can grow into a lifelong contribution to youth sports.

In conclusion, the myth that tee ball teams don't need many assistant coaches couldn't be further from the truth. For safety, effectiveness, individualized instruction, and long-term involvement, assistant coaches are indispensable.

Chapter Review

1. In tee ball, accidents can happen in an instant. Young players love to pick up bats and swing them without realizing the danger. Multiple assistant coaches dramatically reduce risk by ensuring more adults are watching and guiding. Make safety the shared responsibility of every parent on the field.

2. At the very first parents' meeting, set the expectation that every parent is an assistant coach. Use language that

communicates need, not option. The success of the season rests on everyone's participation, not just the head coach.

3. Busy schedules are real, but asking each parent to help with one practice and one game is both fair and manageable. Even small contributions from many adults create a huge collective impact.

4. With enough assistants, you can split your team into smaller groups. This gives players more repetitions, more individualized instruction, and less standing around. Practices run smoother, faster, and with greater fun.

5. Assistant coaches don't need to know baseball. Their first role is safety. Their second is energy. Even parents who know little about the game can chase balls, help set up drills, and encourage kids. With time, they may even grow into strong baseball volunteers.

6. Plant seeds for the future. Sometimes, reluctant parents discover a love of coaching, umpiring, or volunteering because they first dipped a toe into tee ball. That's the "residual effect" — your insistence today could spark lifelong involvement in youth sports.

7. The bigger picture. Coaching tee ball isn't just about teaching kids the basics of the game. It's also about building a community of adults who share responsibility, model teamwork, and create a safe and joyful environment for children. By welcoming many assistant coaches, you're shaping not just this season but the culture of your league.

Coaching Tip

Just because a drill doesn't click with your players one season doesn't mean it's a bad drill. Every group of kids is different—their ages, attention spans, and personalities all affect how well a drill works. Don't be too quick to remove a drill from your list. Keep a running library and revisit it the next year. What fell flat with one group may work beautifully with another.

Sometimes all it takes is a small adjustment: shorten distances, simplify instructions, or add a competitive twist. A drill that once dragged can become one of your best teaching tools when adapted to the players' needs. Coaching is part art, part science: the science is building a toolbox of drills year after year, and the art is knowing when to use them, how to adjust them, and when to shelve them for later. Over time, you'll create not just a list, but a living playbook that grows with you as a coach.

Myth #7: Tee Ball Requires a Perfect Field

Years ago, when I was a young coach in my league, coaching 7 and 8 year-olds, what we used to call the "Rookie League," I organized a practice.

Just a little background. We live in an area called Valley Cottage, New York. We are located 23 miles north of the George Washington Bridge, which connects New Jersey to New York City. Our area borders Nyack, New York. Hence, we are in the Nyack School District. The facilities here are good, with improvements happening all the time. Since my kids graduated from Nyack High School, I have seen a new baseball field built with turf and lights, a new softball field, and a new track surface.

Like many communities the size of Nyack-Valley Cottage, sports have become a popular part of everyone's lives. In fact, there have been numerous professional athletes whose roots began in this area. Most notably: Twins Devin and Jason McCourty, who are both Super Bowl Champions with the New England Patriots. Also, Matt Hennessy and Audric Estimé played or play in the NFL. There have also been a number of other athletes who have succeeded at the college level in other sports. Needless to say every community has its successes it takes pride in. One thing I want to point out is that, at the recreational level, fields and facilities were scarce when I first started coaching youth sports—even with full cooperation from the school district.

Now, back to when I coached rookies. At the time, there was no organization in my local baseball league as far as where and when we were scheduled to practice. This was challenging for someone like me who prided himself on creative practices. It was basically a first-come, first-served kind of survival of the fittest to get a field. I scheduled a practice with my team at a field. When we met there, another team from one of the higher divisions was already practicing. The coach of that team had been in the league for a few years, was successful, and had a reputation as a kind of hothead. One of my assistant coaches volunteered to go over and talk to him about sharing the field. He came back and said there was no way he was moving an inch, and said he was kind of nasty saying it. Now this is where I wish I had more experience as a head coach. I cancelled practice, which I never should have done, and it was a mess getting parents back, being this was before cell phones. I should have handled this differently, but this isn't the end of the story. Jump ahead ten years. I was fortunate to go on an incredible run, winning championships year after year, and I was starting to gain a reputation as a better coach than I probably deserved.

One day, I organized a practice for my 11- and 12-year-old team at a local field. About halfway through, I noticed some very small kids arriving, along with a coach who looked at the field the same way I had looked years earlier—hesitant and uncertain. Remembering my own experience, I decided to take the high road, which ended up paying dividends.

I told my assistant coach to take over our practice, then ran over to the tee ball coach. "Coach," I said, "I only have 30 minutes left, but let's share the field until we're done. How much room do you need?"

After staring in disbelief, he spoke, and we worked out the limited logistics so we could both run meaningful practices. I moved my team over, and we each conducted our sessions. We wrapped up right around the 30 minutes I had mentioned, and on the way out, he expressed his thanks. I reminded him to pay it forward when he coaches 11- and 12-year-olds in the future and to help out the younger teams.

During that practice, one of us—if I recall, it was my team—used half of the basketball court to run drills. I'm not looking for praise or recognition. In fact, some people in my league might describe my coaching style as somewhat... intense.

Coaches and parents involved in youth sports have to adjust to the circumstances that come up. When it comes to field availability, my advice for tee ball coaches is not to be overly concerned with the field and its condition as long as it is safe for the kids. The surface should be flat, and if you have drop-down bases, you can approximate the 45 or 50 feet between them. It is no big deal in practice and in games. Even on a beautiful field, I always take a quick walk around the infield and the outfield. On the nicest fields, I've found broken glass, pens, and even baseballs lodged under the fence. If you spend time as a coach planning your practices, listing the drills you are going to do, the field you use does not have to be manicured like Fenway Park. In the previous chapter, I mentioned that coaches need to have at least one parking lot practice to show their kids their flexibility and creativity.

Solution of Tee Ball Myth #7

The best coaches at any level are flexible and adapt to the talent of their players. Tee ball, in particular, offers the most opportunities when it comes to fields—you don't need a pitcher's mound, marked foul lines, or even dugouts.

When coaching older kids, I emphasize proper fundamentals, like having infielders move their feet toward the ball to field it around the center of their body. Kids sometimes think that a $300 glove will magically make the ball land inside—just as no one becomes a surgeon simply by having the best scalpel.

The same principle applies to fields. Older players benefit from well-maintained fields where bad hops are minimized, but at the tee ball level, a perfect field isn't necessary. In fact, I encourage leagues to reserve the main field for the last two games of the season, giving younger players a goal to earn that privilege.

The best way to counter the "perfect field" myth is to rely on your drill list. Once you've developed 50–100 drills, the need for a pristine field becomes secondary. Always confirm with your league board about any location limitations due to insurance, and remember: safety is the priority. You don't need a gorgeous field to run a productive practice or play a game.

If there's one takeaway from this book—or any of my other resources—it's to open your mind and be creative. Over the years, I've held practices in a variety of unconventional locations, proving that flexibility and imagination matter more than perfection.

1. The town pool parking lot.
2. On the town tennis courts before the nets were put up.
3. In my backyard or that of one of the parents.
4. The cut de sac in my neighborhood.
5. At the state park (inquire about permits)
6. At the town fields (inquire about permits)
7. At the local batting cages.
8. At a school gym.

Now, common sense must prevail. If you are practicing on a black top or concrete, there is no sliding, and you probably have to use tennis balls. The bottom line is that for tee ball, you do not need the perfect field for practice or a game.

Chapter Review

1. Tee ball does not require a pristine, manicured diamond. Coaches who adapt and make use of whatever space is available —parking lots, gyms, backyards, tennis courts—are the ones who create the most meaningful practices.
2. Safety is always prioritized. A flat, debris-free surface matters far more than the condition of the grass. Always do a

quick walk-through of any field or space before practice to spot glass, rocks, or other hazards.

3.   A well-organized drill list makes any practice space effective. The field itself won't make kids better players—your creativity and ability to keep them engaged will.

4.   Be willing to compromise and share fields with other teams. Your players will learn from your example that cooperation, not conflict, is part of the game.

5.   Always confirm with your league whether off-site spaces are covered by insurance, and get the proper permits when required. Flexibility works best when paired with responsibility.

6.   Saving the best field for a "big game" at the end of the season can give young players a sense of accomplishment and motivate them to stick with the program.

7.   Tee ball is not about where you play—it's about how you teach, how you adapt, and how you use every patch of ground as an opportunity to build skills, teamwork, and joy in the game.

Coaching Tip

In youth sports, creativity is one of the most powerful tools a coach can bring. Drills don't always need the same routine—or even the same field. Changing the environment sparks curiosity, energy, and focus. Schedule at least one practice in an unexpected spot—like a parking lot, blacktop, or gym. It may feel unusual, but it teaches kids that the game isn't limited to grass and chalked lines. A parking lot session builds adaptability and sharpens fundamentals without the usual field distractions. Try throwing at a wall or fielding with tennis balls that bounce unpredictably. The lesson goes beyond drills: adjusting to new surroundings builds resilience. A patch of asphalt can become a classroom for creativity, teamwork, and problem-solving. By practicing in different environments, you prepare players not just for the next game, but for challenges anywhere.

Myth #8: There Are No Parental Complaints In Tee Ball

This chapter overlaps with the earlier one on holding a Parents' Meeting, but I want to take a deeper dive here. Why? Because if you continue coaching in youth sports, you're bound to encounter complaints—and sometimes ugly situations—that could be avoided with foresight. Can there really be complaints in tee ball? Absolutely. I know firsthand—not only as a coach and tee ball commissioner who dealt with plenty of them, but also as a tee ball parent who once complained myself. When my middle child played on a neighborhood tee ball team, his coach (a well-meaning neighbor) fell into a bad habit: the same kids played the infield every game, while others were stuck in the outfield game after game. After a while, another parent and I raised the issue. What should have been a constructive conversation turned heated, and I heard explanations that made no sense for 5- and 6-year-old development. The bottom line? I pulled my child off the team and placed him on another one—probably the first midseason transfer in the history of tee ball. It shocked a lot of parents, but I felt it was the fair thing to do.

If you coach at any level in youth sports, you will get complaints. And if you're naturally non-confrontational—as I once was—you'll quickly learn to adapt. Coaching will toughen you, because conflict comes with the territory. One of the biggest complaints often comes before the season even begins. Parents will call insisting their child—let's say Andrea—must be on the same team as her friend Margie. You'll hear every reason in the book: They've always been in the same class. We carpool only with Margie's parents. They won't play unless they're together. Take it from someone who once pulled his own son off a tee ball team: do not allow team-hopping at the tee ball level. As a coach or league administrator, setting that precedent will only come back to haunt you. Tee ball—and youth sports in general—is one of the best opportunities for kids (and parents) to build new friendships. My oldest son was once placed on a tee ball team we wanted him moved from. The league said no. Looking back, it was a blessing. He became best friends with a boy on that team, and that friendship carried all the way into adulthood. They even stood at each other's weddings.

One of the reasons parents will complain about getting their kids on the same team will not be for the kids, but for the parents themselves. They want to talk or gossip with each other while the games or practices are going on. And this brings me to another point about parents watching youth sports. There have been instances where cliques develop or were already established. As a coach, you always want all the parents to feel part of the team. Kids who are friends and parents who are friends are allowed to be separated once in a while. One of the things I always maintained as a youth coach and a parent is to teach flexibility to your kids. You want them to experience new things.

I must address another point of view. In researching this book, I spoke to several tee ball commissioners. Justin, who is the commissioner of a Little League® tee ball league in New York, tries to accommodate parents' wishes, and Justin puts the teams together in March. Interestingly, Justin is going into his second season as commissioner and has yet to field a major complaint, so he is doing a great job! So the theory about changing tee ball teams is purely up to the league.

You will also get complaints about the batting order. Here's a hint that I mentioned before, but it is important and very effective if you go on to coach further in baseball or softball. I have always been adamant about being on time. I developed this system early in my coaching career, where the first person to show up to practice is given number one, the second to show up number two, and so on. This is the order they will bat in batting practice. Simple yet very effective. I would be more flexible in tee ball, but you must keep track of who bats first. For some reason, batting first in tee ball is important to the kids.

Solution of Tee Ball Myth #8

If I am constantly referring to having a Parents' Meeting at the beginning of the season, and it seems I am overselling the idea, well, I am. As I mentioned, this was something I was reluctant to do early in my coaching career, but I learned it was a must for a successful season. And not only at tee ball but with any youth sports team at any level. Remember that a Parents' Meeting will not extinguish all complaints, but it will cut them down. In our area, teams are usually constructed in the Fall before the upcoming season. Here is a quick tip if your league does it that way. Leave one roster spot open per team. This way if there is a family that moves in and is looking for their kids to play tee ball, you will be able to accommodate them. You may even have to have an additional team as you get close to the season. In tee ball, my theory is to accommodate everyone. Do not punish any kids or parents just because they moved into the area one week after the tee ball season started. Get that kid on a team.

Even before the Parents' Meeting, I love to contact every parent with a letter or e-mail. Here is a sample letter I took right from one of my previous books, *T-Ball Skills & Drills*, with a few changes.

Dear T-Ball Player & Parents!

Congratulations on being part of the 2026 Lions tee ball team. My name is Marty Schupak, and I am very excited about coaching my first baseball team. My son, Jeffrey, is five years-old, and he loves baseball and, like me, cannot wait for our season to start. We have a great group of players, and we will be having fun while learning baseball skills. Even though the season is more than three months away, the time will go fast, and before you know it, we will be on the field. Our team is made up of kids whom many of you know already. Here is a list of our roster.

Jack Anderson	*Paula Marks*
Bill Brody	*Bob Nathan*
Edith Clayborn	*Ralph Newman*
Mike Creed	*Barbara Richards*
Larry Fortune	*Jeffrey Schupak*
Dan Jerrius	*Connor Taylor*

Our goal this season will be to see how much we improve as a team from the beginning of the season to the end of the season while having fun. For some of you, like me, this may be your first experience in organized sports, and you might feel a slight bit of nervousness for your child. This is perfectly normal, and I can assure you that the coaches will do everything in our power to make the 2026 tee ball season a positive experience for your child. Along with myself managing the team, we are lucky to have Steve Fortune helping out as a coach. As you know, our league is a volunteer organization, and though coaches enjoy doing it, there are numerous things we may need help with and ask for just a small part of your time during the season.

We will be in touch with you right after the New Year. Until that time, enjoy your winter sports and have a great holiday!

Sincerely,
Marty Schupak
43 Spring Street
Anywhere, New York 10000

(h) 555-5555
E-Mail: baseballcoach_@gmail.com

In this chapter, we are addressing the myth that there are no complaints in tee ball, and you may question what this letter has to do with that. I'm trying to plant positive seeds for the upcoming season and set a certain tone. I'm mentioning something about myself, our goal to improve and have fun, subtly mentioning the need for volunteers, and giving them my complete contact information. All this is very important. After the e-mail, you may get a few phone calls about changing teams, and I highly encourage coaches and leagues not to make any switching of players unless it is necessary. A hint for all youth sports. When you send a letter listing names like above, always do it in alphabetical order. I saw a coach once read off the names of his team in front of a lot of people. As it turns out, he was reading the list of names right from his draft list and the order he drafted his players. A parent figured it out, and it became an ugly situation. Keep names listed on the team roster in alphabetical order.

I follow the previous letter with another one around 7-10 days before the first outdoor practice. It goes something like this:

Dear Lions Tee Ball Parents!

Our season is finally here! We will begin our outdoor practices next week, with our first one being held on Monday, March 19, at Hilltop Middle School at 6 pm sharp. Traditionally, I have a required short parents' meeting with both parents before any player can practice. As someone who works more than one job, I know how tough it is to get everyone together for one meeting. So we will have the parents' meeting at 5:40 pm in the parking lot while my two assistants finish our team practice. The meeting is short, doesn't last more than 15-20 minutes, and I find that going over certain procedures will make for a much smoother season.

Also, I am looking for one parent to be the Lions' team parent. There will be minimal responsibility, like setting up the snack schedule for each game and helping to be in direct contact with parents when we need volunteers. Please contact me if you are interested in being our team parent.

Sincerely,
Marty Schupak
43 Spring Street
Anywhere, New York 10000

(h) 555-5555
E-Mail: baseballcoach_@gmail.com

Again, this letter is another seed for a successful season. For the parents' meeting, refer to the chapter earlier in the book. Parents want someone who is competent and someone who will be a positive role model for their kid(s) for the next 5-6 months.

If you do get a complaint, handle it in the most diplomatic way possible. If you sense a parent is not happy, I have always found that being proactive in the situation is best for all parties. If you have to, call up or approach the parent and say something like:

"Mrs. Cane, I hope your son is enjoying the season, but sometimes I detect a feeling of unhappiness or frustration with you and your husband."

Then just keep quiet and let her respond.

In review, there can be complaints in tee ball. Try to be as organized as possible and make sure you make yourself as accessible as possible. And please have a parents' meeting.

Chapter Review

1. Don't be surprised if you receive complaints. Whether it's about team assignments, batting order, or playing positions, it's part of youth coaching.
2. Communicate early and often. Write at least two letters — one when the team is first formed and another before practices begin. Use these to introduce yourself, set a positive tone, and share important details.
3. Hold a Parents' Meeting. This step may feel unnecessary, but it sets expectations, diffuses potential issues, and helps the season run smoothly. A short, well-run meeting at the very start saves headaches later.
4. Be accessible. Give parents all your contact information. Being approachable shows confidence and prevents frustration from festering in silence.

5. Stay proactive. If you sense a parent is unhappy, reach out early. A calm, respectful conversation often prevents a small concern from growing into a bigger problem.

6. Model flexibility. Just as kids need to learn to adapt — playing with new teammates, taking turns in different spots — parents also benefit from seeing flexibility encouraged as part of the tee ball experience.

7. The key takeaway: complaints are not proof of failure; they are proof you're coaching real families with real concerns. By being organized, approachable, and proactive, you not only manage complaints but turn them into opportunities for stronger connections and a better season for everyone.

Coaching Tip

Playing only one sport year-round may seem like a shortcut to skill, but it comes with risks: overuse injuries, burnout, and limited overall athletic development. Experts recommend delaying specialization until at least age 14. Encourage kids to play multiple sports each season and take meaningful off-seasons — variety builds versatility, keeps them engaged, and fosters a lifelong love of play.

Myth #9: Tee Ball Is Only For Future Baseball & Softball Players

The idea that tee ball is only for future baseball and softball players is not true. Some major league baseball players who didn't start playing until later in their lives have expressed that they would have loved to start playing earlier than they did. Hall of Fame pitcher Randy Johnson admits baseball was not his first love growing up, and he didn't take the game seriously until later on in his teenage years. Both Matt Kemp and Dee Gordon, successful MLB players, started playing baseball later than their peers.

Tee ball is meant to serve as a developmental and introductory sport with an emphasis on fun for young children. While some say tee ball teaches baseball skills, I like to say it exposes them to baseball skills. Parents should encourage their own kids who have shown no interest in baseball or softball to at least try tee ball. Besides enhancing children's gross and fine motor skills, the social aspect will encourage new short-term and long-term friendships. When we were children, we were all in situations where we didn't want to do or try something different, when our parents would insist we try it! And sometimes we liked it, and sometimes we didn't like it. Tee ball can be and is a great activity for 5 and 6 year-old baseball lovers and non-lovers. If the coach prepares stimulating drills and upbeat practices, most young kids will enjoy tee ball. To narrow it down to only baseball and softball lovers would be a crime. Is there a chance that a young boy or girl who didn't want to play tee ball has a good time? Of course. Can a young boy or girl develop a liking for baseball or softball after a tee ball season? Absolutely! Parents who are looking for activities for their young kids need to consider tee ball just as they consider piano lessons, dance, and swimming.

Some parents or coaches might say, "If your child isn't serious about baseball, don't bother with tee ball." This thinking misses the point. Tee ball is about growth, not grooming future stars. While tee ball can help children transition into coach-pitch baseball or softball, it is designed to meet kids where they are developmentally. Kids move on when ready and interested. Not all players go on to pursue baseball seriously, nor is that the only valuable outcome. To sum it up, tee ball is much more than just a preparatory stage for future baseball or softball players; it is a foundational activity that supports children's physical, social, and emotional development through fun and learning at an early age.

And the emphasis must be on fun. Tee ball is for every child, not just future ball players. It's a playful, developmental activity that can benefit any child, regardless of whether they ever step on a baseball diamond again. Plus, tee ball encourages a love for the game.

Solution of Tee Ball Myth #9

Tee ball coaches and leagues can be the ones to help dismiss the myth that tee ball is only for future ball players. When I first moved into my community, the realtor gave us a packet. I think they called it a Welcome Wagon. In it was information about the community we moved into. Valuable information about our volunteer fire department, the local library hours, and other such items, which I thought was great. But there was nothing about the local recreational sports leagues. When I got on my local Little League® Board of Directors, I made it a point to have our information about joining our league in this Welcome Wagon. Though everything is now on the Internet, it behooves local sports leagues to have some kind of introduction to the area and what youth sports are available, and who to contact. In doing so, I would actually separate the baseball information into two categories, with one encompassing everything about the league, including tee ball, and another just about tee ball. Have a separate flyer that has a headline for the tee ball program, something like this:

"You Don't Have To Be A Home Run Hitter To Play In Our All-Inclusive Tee Ball Program."

And have 4 or 5 pictures of kids doing tee ball activities. And most of all, list who to contact. It is good branding to emphasize the tee ball program alone. You want parents to encourage their kids to try it. Many times, some parents have had a bad experience in sports while growing up. They can have the attitude that "I'm never going to have my kids go through what I went through." For some reason, the father, for instance, was embarrassed on the baseball field as a kid; you want him to kind of think that tee ball is different from the baseball experience he went through. Remember that there is some selling and marketing in recruiting new players.

In addition to the Welcome Wagon idea, the league website should include what some of the goals are in the league's tee ball program. I've come up with the following:

Goals of the Tee Ball Program

<u>1. Emphasis on Fun and Participation</u>
- Ensure every child has an enjoyable experience regardless of skill level.
- Making the experience enjoyable enough that children want to continue playing sports.
- Promote equal playing time and frequent engagement for all players.
- Encourage teamwork, communication, and respect for teammates and coaches.

2. Building Confidence and Self-Esteem
* Building self-confidence and self-esteem through participation and achievement.
  * Celebrate small victories and effort, not just performance.
  * Create an environment where players feel safe to try, fail, and improve.

3. Introduction to the Game of Baseball
  * Teach basic rules and concepts in a fun and engaging way.
  * Introduce the field layout, positions, and purpose of each.

4. Introducing Good Sportsmanship
  * Teach respect for opponents, coaches, umpires, and the game itself.
  * Reinforce the value of playing fair and being a gracious teammate and opponent.

5. Family Involvement
  * Encourage family support on and off the field.
  * Create opportunities for parents to volunteer and stay connected.

6. Preparing for the Next Level
  * Lay the foundation for moving up to coach-pitch and beyond.
  * Begin to introduce concepts like positions and simple plays in a gradual, age-appropriate way.

7. Overall Program Goals
  * Tee ball should emphasize fun, fitness, and fundamentals in a positive, supportive environment that encourages both players

and coaches to return through enjoyable early baseball experiences.

The information I listed above as the goals of the tee ball program is less than 300 words. If you notice, I don't get into the meat and potatoes of what we want to do with regard to baseball until number three. Remember, we want to promote the tee ball program as a special program for activities for kids that will be fun while exposing them to baseball. From the outline I listed, there may be some brushback from the pure baseball parent who played in high school and college, and he might ask the league, "Is there any baseball being taught in this program?" We can address this easily by showing the parents all the championship banners and trophies the league earned. Trust me as someone who is as competitive as they come. There will be a time for fierce competition, but tee ball is not the place.

Another way to dispel this myth, as I've emphasized before, is to approach the season as part physical education teacher and part tee ball coach. If your practices keep kids active, engaged, and having fun, both your reputation and the league's will naturally grow. Word will spread through friends and neighbors that the local tee ball program is outstanding, and parents will encourage others to join.

In the end, the idea that tee ball is only for future baseball or softball players is simply not true. Everyone should be encouraged to give it a try! And as coaches, we must remember that we are ambassadors of the game—representing baseball and softball in the best way possible.

Chapter Review

1.   Tee ball is for everyone. One of the biggest myths is that tee ball is only meant for kids who will eventually play baseball or softball. In truth, tee ball should be presented as an inclusive, introductory activity where every child—regardless of background, athletic ability, or future interest—can participate and have fun.

2.   Community awareness matters. Families moving into a new area may not know about local youth sports opportunities. Just as a "Welcome Wagon" shares important community information, leagues should make sure new residents can easily find details about how to join. Flyers, welcome packets, and clear contact information all help build awareness.

3.   Promote tee ball separately. Don't let tee ball get buried under the larger baseball program. Market it as its own offering, with its own flyer, images, and message. Highlight that kids don't need to be "home run hitters" to join. Branding tee ball separately helps reach parents who might otherwise assume it's too competitive or too advanced.

4.   Share program goals publicly. League websites and handouts should list the specific goals of the tee ball program. Emphasize fun, participation, teamwork, confidence-building, and family involvement before mentioning baseball-specific skills. This reassures parents that tee ball is designed to be a positive experience, not an early grind toward competition.

5.   Address concerns from "serious" baseball parents. Some parents may ask, "But when will they actually learn baseball?" Leagues can confidently point to their track record of developing players over time, while reminding parents that tee ball is a foundation. The competitive side will come later — this stage is about fun and learning.

6. Coaches as ambassadors. Every tee ball coach should see themselves not just as a teacher of skills, but also as a promoter of youth sports in the community. A fun, stimulating tee ball experience becomes the best advertisement, as parents spread the word and recommend the program to friends and neighbors.

Coaching Tip

Even at the tee ball level, warming up isn't just a formality—it's a foundational habit that sets kids up for safety, confidence, and enjoyment. A simple 5–10 minute warm-up routine helps prepare young muscles and joints for activity, lowers the risk of injury, and gets kids mentally ready to play. Research in youth sports shows that consistent warm-ups improve coordination and reduce injury rates in children by as much as 30%. At this age, the warm-up doesn't need to be complicated: jogging the bases, light stretches, or fun movement games are enough to activate their bodies. Establishing this routine early teaches kids that preparation is part of playing, a lesson that will carry over as they grow into more competitive levels of the game.

Myth #10: The Tee Ball Rule Book Must Be Followed

This myth, I can write a separate book on. Leagues have a charter, which is necessary for leagues to exist, and certain rules must be followed. For instance, all batting helmets used must meet the specifications of the National Operating Committee on Standards for Athletic Equipment (NOCSAE) and bear the NOCSAE stamp. This is the fundamental requirement ensuring the helmet meets specific safety standards. Now this is a good rule. No matter the sport, safety trumps all. Whether it is a 5 year-old tee ball player or a college All-American, or a shortstop with the Dodgers, safety rules must be followed. And these safety rules are not only for players but for coaches. I remember coaching one of my teams one year from the third base coaching box. As some of you will discover, standing there often means negotiating foul balls —sometimes catching the softer ones, other times dodging the harder shots with a quick "Tennessee two-step." But the longer you coach, the more you realize your reflexes aren't what they used to be, and those hard-hit fouls get a lot tougher to avoid. Then, on July 22, 2007, an incident happened that truly changed me. It occurred during the ninth inning of a Texas League minor league game between the Tulsa Drillers and the Arkansas Travelers in North Little Rock, Arkansas. Mike Coolbaugh, just 35 years old, was serving as the first base coach for the Tulsa Drillers, a Double-A affiliate of the Colorado Rockies. A screaming line-drive foul ball struck Coach Coolbaugh in the neck, crushing his left vertebral artery. The impact caused a massive brain hemorrhage, and despite immediate medical attention and prolonged CPR efforts, he was tragically pronounced dead at 9:47 p.m. that same night. The event shocked the baseball community at every level, serving as a heartbreaking reminder that the game we love carries real risks not only for players but also for coaches and anyone close to the field of play. In the wake of this incident, Major League Baseball made an important change, mandating that all base coaches wear protective helmets starting with the 2008 season. For some, it may have seemed like a small adjustment, but for those of us who coach, the reasoning was clear and powerful — safety should never be taken lightly, no matter how routine the role may feel. From that point on, I began wearing a helmet every time I coached from the third base box and insisted that any of my assistants do the same when they filled in for me. It's worth noting that in the tragic case of Coach Coolbaugh, the blow was not to the head itself, but the incident served as a sobering reminder that freak accidents can and do happen without warning. Reducing the odds, even slightly, that a coach might be injured above the shoulders is worth the small inconvenience of wearing protective gear. Baseball is full of traditions, but when safety is at stake, adapting should always come first. This rule is not only good, it's necessary, and I strongly recommend that all coaches wear helmets, regardless of whether their league requires it or not.

I want to address a few issues that are in many tee ball league rule books and then give alternatives so we don't have to follow the tee ball rule book exactly as it is laid out.

1) When I coached my oldest son in tee ball, the league had a rule: if a player couldn't hit the ball off the tee after five swings, you moved on to the next batter to keep the game moving. WRONG! Never leave a tee ball player standing at the tee in front of a crowd of parents and kids having just experienced failure. In tee ball, every player must experience success. (And this is strictly for tee ball.) How do we make that happen? I'll address that in the solution section. Just remember—once players move up to the next level with pitching, they'll naturally learn how to handle both success and failure.

In tee ball, putting players in a position to succeed is one of the most important responsibilities of a coach and parent — not only for skill development but also for confidence and long-term interest in the game. When a child experiences success (making contact, catching a ball, running to the right base), even small successes, it builds their self-esteem and confidence. It's not just important; it's foundational to everything else you do as a tee ball coach. After I witnessed over the course of the tee ball season some players being removed after their fifth swing, I decided to make changes.

2) Another issue is the number of players that are on a tee ball roster. The smaller team size compared to older baseball divisions ensures that each child gets plenty of at-bats and defensive playing time, keeps games shorter, and helps maintain engagement and fun for young players. The problem is that a lot of leagues will have up to 14 players on a roster. There are numerous issues involved with an overweight roster filled with too many bodies.

3) What about gloves? Did you ever go into one of those big box department stores, and in the sports goods section, you see a package that says: *Official Tee Ball Glove.*

Did you ever take a close look at the glove? It's something I like to call a pancake glove. I challenge any 5 or 6 year-old to actually catch a fly ball with that glove. Besides, I've been involved in baseball for a long time. I don't know of any universal official baseball glove. Though there is no rule that says a player must wear a glove, it's considered essential equipment for participation.

I have a different theory, which I will get to in the solution section. But I just want to share a story that might help you out when you are in the market for baseball or softball equipment for your kids. When you need gloves, bats, etc., before you go out and spend hundreds of dollars buying the equipment, try this. One Saturday, take your kids around the neighborhood and knock on doors—especially at houses where you know the kids are grown. Bring along a simple flyer with your phone number. When someone answers, just explain that your kids are getting started in youth sports and ask if they have any old equipment they'd like to part with. Trust me, this works! If it's a mom whose children are long out of the house, don't be surprised if she says she's been waiting for someone like you for years. Before you know it, she'll be leading you to the basement or garage and telling you to take what you need. I know, because we did it—and even came home with a good bike.

We are a nation with rules, and lately we keep hearing the term "Rule of Law," but I want to show why tee ball leagues need flexibility in the rules, not counting the safety rules, for the betterment of the players. I will address in the next section the three issues I brought up: the five swings, the number of players on a team, and the tee ball glove.

Solution of Tee Ball Myth #10

The myth that the tee ball rule book must be followed should not be followed. I'm not telling you to throw it out. As I mentioned, safety trumps everything, so you must adhere to all the safety rules put in place. I'm just trying to give tee ball commissioners and coaches flexibility so 100% of the kids can experience success.

Let's take a look at the three examples I gave: 1) only 5 swings allowed per at bat, 2) the number of players on a team, 3) players' gloves.

The worst thing we can do as leagues, coaches, and parents is remove players from their at-bat simply because they didn't experience success. A child's chances of returning the next year—or even continuing in youth sports at all—can be diminished depending on how sensitive the player is. But what are the options?

First, remember that I'm specifically referring to tee ball for 5- and 6-year-olds. Nationally, tee ball leagues often include kids ages 4–7. With that in mind, the options are plentiful if we put on our creative hats. Today, there are balls of all different sizes and materials. Leagues should have several on hand. If a player misses three times, switch to a larger ball that's still safe. If he misses on the fourth swing, try the old Marty Schupak tee ball plunger system: place a short, new, clean bathroom plunger into the batting tee with a large, safe ball balanced on top. The player will hit the bigger ball and feel successful. Common sense should always prevail when working with kids. Leagues should not be hamstrung by a requirement to use the "official" tee ball 100% of the time. We have to be willing to deviate from those types of rules for the benefit of all players.

With the growing number of players on a team, leagues are sometimes caught in a tough situation. There are always late registrations, families moving into the area, and other circumstances where players might be left out if rosters are set too early. Let me state clearly that tee ball rosters should not be finalized until right before the season starts. Some leagues set teams and keep adding new registrants until opening day, and while that can work, I've seen rosters balloon to as many as 14 kids. Those games drag on, with players getting fewer chances at bat or in the field. My suggestion—though not in any rule book—is to split teams in half for most of the season and run two games simultaneously with fewer players per side. For example, if one team has 12 players and the other has 10, divide them so it's 6 versus 5 on two separate fields. Players will get twice as many opportunities, and you can extend games from three innings to four or even five. If teams play ten games, use this format for eight of them. Keep one full-roster game at midseason and another for the finale. You can also split it evenly—five and five—if you prefer.

Remember, in tee ball you can always use drop-down bases and create a field almost anywhere.

The third example I gave about players using gloves is interesting. I'm a huge believer in doing some fielding drills without gloves at almost all levels with the appropriate type of baseballs. Let me explain. Early in my coaching career, I noticed a troubling habit with some kids when teaching them to catch ground balls. Some players tended to move their feet less and reach more with their glove hand. I came up with my own theory. I'll repeat the story I mentioned earlier, that some players think that because their parents bought them a three-hundred-dollar baseball glove, the ball would automatically find its way into it. I began to install bare-handed fielding drills with softer baseballs. Players moved their feet better and faster, knowing that the closer the ball lined up to the center of the body, the better the chance of fielding the ground ball. For tee ball I would have the kids play the first one or two games bare-handed with the appropriate ball. Doing this, we are not having the players develop a dependency on their gloves and are getting kids into the habit of moving their feet.

These are just three examples that leagues should consider.

The purpose of a tee ball rulebook is to provide a clear, consistent, and age-appropriate set of guidelines for how the game should be played.

In summary, the tee ball rulebook's primary purpose is to provide structure that makes the game safe, fair, and enjoyable for young children learning the basics of baseball, while also helping coaches and parents create a positive early sports experience. My argument is that if safety is not compromised, shouldn't a coach and league have the flexibility to deviate from their rules so the player achieves success? My answer is yes. Coaches in tee ball should have significant flexibility to deviate from strict interpretations of the rulebook when it directly benefits the player's development, engagement, and enjoyment, and does not compromise safety or the fundamental spirit of the game. You won't find a rule that says " Tee ball players shall be ejected if they do not wear a glove."

Leagues need to set up their own rules to benefit the players. Keep in mind that because of field logistics, a tee ball game in Des Moines, Iowa, might have to be set a little differently from a game in New York City. Also, the fact that tee ball can encompass ages 4-7 means leagues have to have the ability to be flexible and adjust. And I say that there have to be in-game adjustments just so the players has a chance to feel better about themselves.

So I am urging all league presidents to please give your tee ball commissioner and team managers the ability to change things on the fly for the betterment of the kids. Tee ball rule books should not be followed to the "t" as long as safety is not compromised!

A quick addition: I came across another clever idea from a tee ball commissioner — also named Justin, coincidentally, though this one is from New Jersey. He introduced a fun and creative rule where the last hitter in the lineup is designated the "Home Run Hitter." When it's that player's turn, the coaches place runners on all the bases, the batter hits the ball off the tee, and then circles the bases for a grand slam home run.

It's such a simple adjustment, but the impact is huge. Instead of feeling like an afterthought at the bottom of the order, the last batter suddenly becomes the star of the inning. What could easily feel like a negative — being the "last up" — is transformed into an exciting moment. Every child gets the thrill of hitting a guaranteed grand slam, and the whole team shares in the celebration as they cheer the runner around the bases.

This kind of creative thinking is exactly what youth sports need more of. It keeps kids smiling, engaged, and excited to return to the field the following week. By turning routine moments into highlights not found in the rulebook, commissioners and coaches can spark enthusiasm while fostering a love of the game that lasts well beyond the tee ball years.

Chapter Review

1.   The rulebook provides structure and safety, but should not be applied rigidly. Rules exist to guide the game and keep it safe, but tee ball is meant as an entry point to baseball, not a strict competition. Coaches should view the rulebook as a framework, not a checklist that must be followed word for word.

2.   Safety rules (e.g., certified helmets) are always non-negotiable. Equipment standards, like using NOCSAE-approved helmets, are critical and must always be enforced. These safeguards protect children and ensure parents feel confident about their child's well-being on the field.

3.   Overly strict rules—such as five-swing strikeouts or oversized rosters — can discourage players. Young children can easily become frustrated or embarrassed if rules are applied too harshly. Keeping rosters manageable and allowing flexibility in batting or fielding helps every child feel included.

4.   Coaches should adapt rules to fit the kids' needs, building confidence and keeping practices fun. Adjustments — such as letting a child swing until they hit or giving everyone a turn in the field — create an atmosphere of encouragement. This flexibility keeps kids engaged and reduces early dropouts.

5.   Creative adjustments (larger balls, bare-handed fielding, smaller groups) enhance skill development. Modifying equipment and drills to match the players' abilities allows them to develop fundamental skills at their own pace. These creative tweaks keep the focus on learning rather than strict adherence to rules.

6. Tee ball's goal is inclusion, enjoyment, and learning—not strict enforcement of every regulation. The heart of the program is giving children a positive first sports experience. Rules should support — not overshadow — those goals.

7. Leagues should empower coaches to be flexible while always prioritizing safety. Boards and directors should reinforce that safety is mandatory, but creativity is encouraged. When coaches feel supported, they can make decisions that keep the program fun and welcoming.

Coaching Tip

Recovery is training too. Older youth athletes often push hard in games and practices, giving maximum effort in drills and workouts. But without proper rest, stretching, hydration, and especially quality sleep, all that hard work can backfire. Teaching athletes to balance fierce training with recovery prevents injuries, reduces burnout, and improves performance. Establishing these habits now builds lifelong routines that keep players strong, healthy, and performing at their best both on and off the field.

Chapter 3

Some of My Favorite Tee Ball Drills

In this section, I'm sharing some of my most popular and effective tee ball drills—ones that have stood the test of time from my previous books. These drills have been proven to engage young players, build fundamental skills, and keep practices fun. If you're looking for even more ideas, check your local library for resources like T-Ball Drills and T-Ball Skills and Drills. I'm working to make as many of these resources available for free as possible, so libraries are an excellent starting point.

A well-structured practice should last anywhere from 45 to 60 minutes—no longer. You can be the most creative tee ball coach in the world, but if practices run too long, you'll lose the attention and enthusiasm of many players. Within that 45-60 minute window, plan for about six drills, with one or two alternates in case you need variety or a quick change of pace. A good balance is four skill-building drills and two fun drills or games to keep energy high. A sample practice schedule might look like this:

5–10 minutes – Baseball skill drill
5–10 minutes – Baseball skill drill
5–10 minutes – Fun game
5–10 minutes – Baseball skill drill
5–10 minutes – Baseball skill drill
5–10 minutes – Fun game

This schedule is not set in stone. Some groups may handle a 15-minute skill session without issue, while others may need more frequent breaks and variety to stay engaged. The key is observation: watch the kids' energy levels, attention spans, and enthusiasm. Be ready to adjust on the fly, swap drills, or take short breaks when needed. Flexibility is essential to keeping practices productive, positive, and enjoyable.

By preparing a clear plan ahead of time and balancing skill development with fun, you'll create a practice environment that fosters learning, confidence, and most importantly, a love of the game that keeps kids coming back week after week.

Things to Keep in Mind

1. Skill Level Over Age: If the team varies widely in ability, it's often more effective to divide kids by skill level rather than age for certain drills. This gives every child the chance to succeed and grow at their own pace.

2. Short and Positive: Keep drills short and positive. Kids respond well to encouragement and will remember how they felt more than what they were taught.

3. End on a High Note: Always wrap up practice with a fun game or a team celebration. There's nothing better than seeing every child leave the field smiling and excited to come back.

#1 Multiple Object Throw Drill

THE SET-UP

We use a variety of objects—baseballs, bean bags, yarn balls, plastic bottles, and rags tied in knots. Spread the players out, give each one a bucket, and have them practice throwing their objects into open space.

WHO IS THIS DRILL GOOD FOR?

It is especially good for first-time tee ball players. Some will try throwing each object the same way.

WHY IS IT BENEFICIAL?

Giving first-time tee ball players different projectiles is a great idea. Most players will throw the object the same way, but others will subtly adjust their throw. This is exposing players to throwing objects of different sizes and weights.

COMMENTS:

Make sure players are spread out. Use this drill as one station. It's helpful to place a cone beyond each player as a target, which encourages proper head positioning and helps prevent the objects from scattering. Early in the season, focus on one skill at a time: if you're teaching throwing, don't combine it with catching; if you're teaching catching, don't have them throw.

#2 Free Standing Bench Throw Drill

THE SET-UP

Use a free-standing bench for this drill. Have the player lie down on the bench while the coach or parent stands at the foot. The player holds a safe object—such as a Nerf ball, tennis ball, or rag ball—brings their arm down, then up, and throws the object to the person standing at the end of the bench.

WHO IS THIS DRILL GOOD FOR?

Many young players don't bring their arms back when throwing. This is good for new tee ball players and those who have been spotted not bringing their arms back when throwing.

WHY IS IT BENEFICIAL?

Players will practice throwing while being coached to bring their throwing arm back. Even if they aren't doing it correctly on their own, they often believe they are. Using the bench allows gravity to naturally guide the arm back, helping players feel the proper motion for the first time.

COMMENTS:

Even though the coach or parent stands at the foot of the bench, the player's throw may not land perfectly, and that's okay—the main goal is for the player to feel the arm moving back. There's no need to buy a bench if you don't have one;

the ends of metal bleachers work just as well. Repeating this drill multiple times helps the player develop muscle memory.

#3 Four Square Step And Throw Drill

THE SET-UP

If you become motivated and industrious, this is a great drill to organize. Take four sheets of oak tag and cut out a square in each one with a 2"-4" border. A sharp utility knife will work.

WHO IS THIS DRILL GOOD FOR?

This is good for first-year tee ball players when combining stepping and throwing.

WHY IS IT BENEFICIAL?

All kids have different athletic abilities. This template might help those players who have the right throwing technique with their arm, but below the waist, their legs may not be moving correctly.

COMMENTS:

If you want to invest a little, you can have the squares laminated. Start by having players throw without the square, then estimate the appropriate distance for each. Every player's square placement will differ. Combining stepping and throwing can be challenging in this setup. Keep in mind that motor skills vary among kids. It's crucial to have them practice the throwing motion without a ball at first. Some will still struggle, but if they develop a rhythmic motion, they'll be set up for success. This isn't an exact science, but the hands-on experience with the steps makes this drill worthwhile.

#4 Over-Under Throwing Drill

THE SET-UP

We put blue masking tape in a straight line going across a fence. Soft-covered balls are used. You can use rag balls. Each player holds a ball (or other object) and the coach yells instructions with "over" or "under," and the player(s) must try to throw the ball above or below the line, depending on the command.

WHO IS THIS DRILL GOOD FOR?

This is an excellent drill for first-year tee ball players, though I wouldn't do it at the first practice. Maybe about a third into the season. Coaches can judge when to use it.

WHY IS IT BENEFICIAL?

This drill combines a physical action with a mental focus, challenging players while keeping the task achievable. The blue tape serves as a target, helping players keep their heads steady and reducing errant throws.

COMMENTS:

Make sure your league allows a drill like this. Some facility managers don't permit even lightweight objects to be thrown at their fences. You can also use a concrete wall and mark the over-under line with chalk. Be sure to spread the players out. This drill works well as a station, ideally with only one or two throwers at a time.

#5 Line Throw Drill

THE SET-UP

Line up two rows of baseballs in front of the third base and shortstop positions. Players form a line behind each row. The first player at third base runs to the nearest ball and throws it to first base, then moves to the end of the other line. Next, the first player at shortstop does the same, throwing the ball and then joining the end of the opposite line.

WHO IS THIS DRILL GOOD FOR?

This is one of my staple warm-up drills for older kids. It is good for tee ball players because it teaches the concept of throwing the ball to first base.

WHY IS IT BENEFICIAL?

The players are being conditioned in a good way. They are learning basic baseball fundamentals in a non-threatening way. It is also a beneficial drill because players receive multiple repetitions within a short period of time. While station drills with small groups of kids work well, experiencing a drill with the whole team is valuable.

COMMENTS:

Emphasize to the players that they don't have to reach first base on a fly, especially early in the season. Accuracy rather than distance is preferred. Use a coach at first base; he presents a larger target. With older kids, I use another player at first base, which you can try during the season.

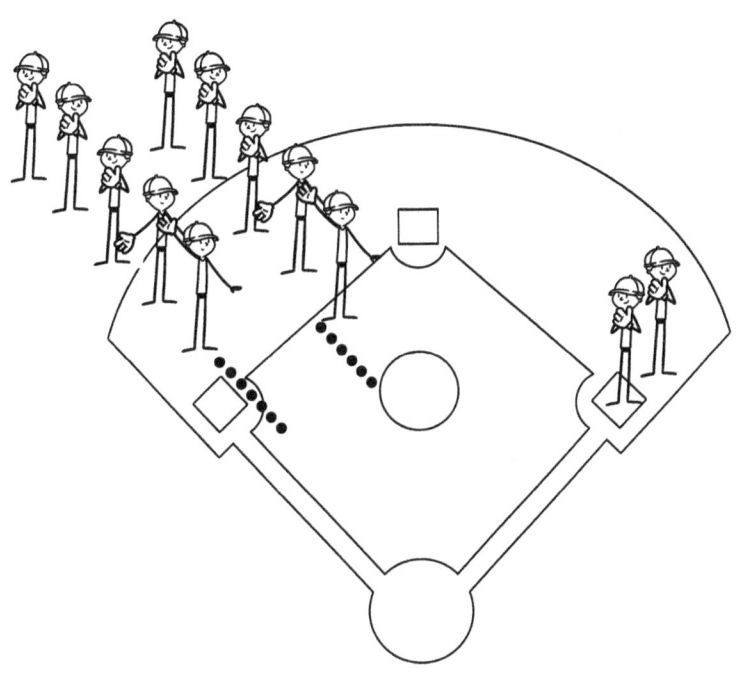

#6 Baseball Golf Drill

THE SET-UP

We set up three lightweight cones on a field. It is preferable to put the cone on top of a three-box pyramid to make the target easier to hit. A group of two or three kids with a coach is grouped together. They will move from cone to cone, trying to throw a ball and knock down each cone.

WHO IS THIS DRILL GOOD FOR?

This drill could be tough for the youngest tee ball players. However, I like to try this with all the kids. When they do knock down the cone (on the boxes), the reaction from them is just like they hit a home run over the fence.

WHY IS IT BENEFICIAL?

We are putting the drill of throwing into a game. This is a great way to break up a practice. And if done at the end of practice, the kids leave on a high note. Also, this is a great at-home drill.

COMMENTS:

You can keep track of the number of throws, like in golf, but try to keep it non-competitive. You must break up the team into, say, three or four different groups. Try and teach the concept to the kids, not to try reaching the cone on one throw. Also, tell the kids they do not have to knock down the cone on a fly.

#7 Scatch Fly Ball Drill

THE SET-UP

One of the few drills I recommend that you spend some money. But I have found this drill very worthwhile. We use what I remembered they named Scatch. It is a kind of paddle that has a strap behind it, and the hand goes through to control it. The paddle has a velcro surface, accompanied by a velcro ball. You can purchase as many pairs as your budget allows.

WHO IS THIS DRILL GOOD FOR?

This is a great drill for all tee ball players to help gain confidence catching fly balls. It is also fun in that kids love to use different props, and this one scores well with the kids. This is a great station drill during a tee ball practice as well as a great at-home drill.

WHY IS IT BENEFICIAL?

Too many times, tee ball coaches will begin having the kids catch a ball when some have no concept of how to do it. If the player gets injured early in tee ball, it may be tough to get them back on the field. This drill will enrich players' confidence.

COMMENTS:

Start the distance short. You can also start by throwing underhanded to the kids. If a player is very nervous and reluctant, have him feel the velcro ball so he knows it is an item that you most likely will not get hurt from.

#8 Scoop Ball Drill

THE SET-UP

Take two empty one-gallon plastic milk containers. With a utility knife, cut off about 1/3rd of the bottom. Don't worry if it isn't exactly even. After you cut it, the exposed edge will be sharp. Line it with duct tape. This is to prevent any type of cuts or injuries. Then take a rag ball, which is a clean rag, rolled up into a knot, covered with one-inch and two-inch masking tape. Have a one-on-one catch with a player or your son or daughter.

WHO IS THIS DRILL GOOD FOR?

This is a very good exercise for young kids. I have done this with kids as young as four years old. It probably works best with kids ages five and up.

WHY IS IT BENEFICIAL?

This is an alternative to using a glove. We all buy our kids things. We are showing kids some creativity. Another benefit is that when you create it with your son or daughter, the quality time will be remembered by them for a long time, well past tee ball.

COMMENTS:

If your son or daughter masters this drill, try it with half-gallon milk containers. You can use plastic balls, but they have a tendency to bounce out. An alternative is taking a kitchen garbage bag. Throw the rag ball to your child and see if they can direct the ball into the bag while they are holding it open.

#9 Color Code Ball Recognition Drill

THE SET-UP

Use a few soft, non-threatening baseballs and color-code them. I usually apply colored circle stickers about the size of a quarter, which you can find at a stationery store. You could also use a colored Sharpie, but I prefer to avoid permanent ink. Each ball should have two marks of the same color—one might be blue, another red, yellow, and so on. As you throw ground balls, the player shouts out the color as soon as they see it while fielding, saying "blue" or "red" as the ball goes into their glove.

WHO IS THIS DRILL GOOD FOR?

This is a great drill and one of my favorites. It is good for any age child starting at around five years old.

WHY IS IT BENEFICIAL?

At all levels of baseball, fielders tend to lift their heads too soon. This is especially true at the higher levels with potential double plays and the anxiousness to "get two". Conditioning kids at a young age to keep their heads down and watch the ball go into the glove or their bare hands is good fundamentals. This should be reinforced at all levels of play.

COMMENTS:

I love this drill and begin with the fielders using only their bare hands. Afterward, we transition to gloves. This is a one-skill drill, focusing solely on catching. After making the catch, the player simply flips the ball aside without throwing it.

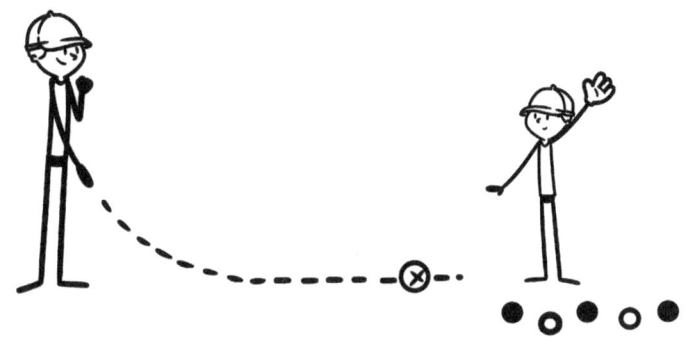

#10 Goalie Drill

THE SET-UP

Two cones are set up ten to fifteen feet apart, depending on the age and ability of the player. One player stands between the two cones. The coach throws ground balls between the cones. The player has to keep the ball from getting behind him.

WHO IS THIS DRILL GOOD FOR?

Any age player, and if you continue coaching in the higher levels, consider continuing to do this drill.

WHY IS IT BENEFICIAL?

The main concept to try to get across, which may be difficult for tee ball players to understand, is to block the ball, trying to keep it in front of you. A play can still be made.

COMMENTS:

I like the players to do this drill bare-handed at the beginning and then transition to using gloves. Feel free to adjust the width of the cones, making it wider or narrower. Coaches or parents can slow down or speed up the tempo of the drill depending on the player. I've done this drill with high school age kids, hitting the ball really fast-paced, and it becomes a dual-purpose drill, also working on conditioning.

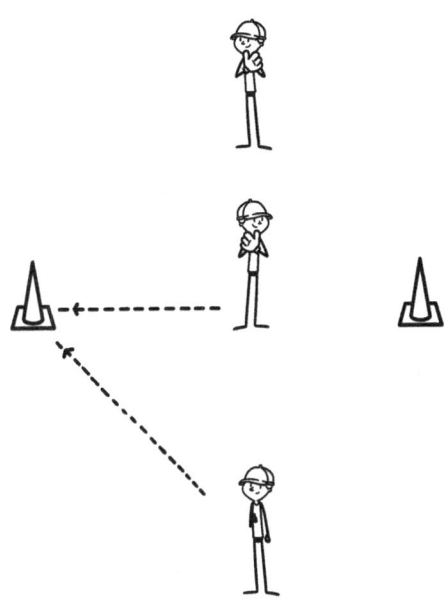

#11 Turn Drill

THE SET-UP

Two players stand about 15-20 feet from the coach, spread out about 10 feet apart. Both players' backs are to the coach. The one player goes first, and the coach throws a ground ball. When the coach yells "Turn," that player turns around and tries to catch the ball.

WHO IS THIS DRILL GOOD FOR?

This is an excellent drill for all ages.

WHY IS IT BENEFICIAL?

We are viewing the players' reaction time while also exercising their hand-eye coordination. Drills targeting reaction time improve athletic skills, cognitive processing, and overall performance. This drill helps lay the groundwork for higher-level play and overall physical literacy.

COMMENTS:

After each player takes a turn, they don't throw the ball back but roll it to the side. I like to start this drill bare-handed, then transition to gloves. Coaches should emphasize catching, but stopping the ball is equally valuable. Adjust the drill's pace and throw speed for each player. Stick to ground balls, though with older kids, line drives can be used. Always use soft-covered balls.

#12 Circle Drill

THE SET-UP

The players form a circle. When the coach yells "Go," they throw a ground ball to one player in the circle. If that player catches it, they then throw it to anyone in the circle—just not to the players immediately to their left or right.

WHO IS THIS DRILL GOOD FOR?

The is a good mid-season drill for tee ball players.

WHY IS IT BENEFICIAL?

This drill can be challenging for tee ball players to follow precisely. In tee ball, learning to follow instructions is just as important as swinging a bat or catching a ball. It's the glue that makes coaching, teamwork, and fun happen safely and effectively. In this drill, keeping the head down on ground balls is equally important as following directions.

COMMENTS:

This drill will likely work better in the middle of the season rather than during the first or second practice. A bigger challenge, which may be too difficult for tee ball players, is using two baseballs at once. With older teams, I sometimes split them into two separate circles and make it a competition to see how many balls can be caught without an error. I like to start this drill bare-handed, using the appropriate soft-covered ball.

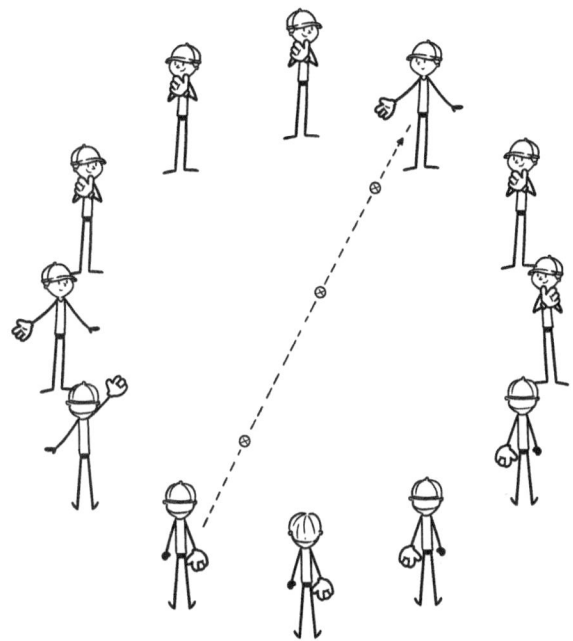

#13 Bubble Hit Drill

THE SET-UP

This one is easy — a container of bubbles, a big red plastic bat. Alternatives can be an old tennis racquet or anything a young child can hold comfortably and move.

WHO IS THIS DRILL GOOD FOR?

You may want to ask, how young is too young to introduce hitting? If you are like I was when my kids were young, almost right out of the crib, I did this little exercise, and they all loved it. Pick and choose when you want to try this. There is no minimum or maximum age limit to the fun they'll have with this drill.

WHY IS IT BENEFICIAL?

Hand-eye coordination development begins very early in infancy and continues to refine significantly through childhood. I could give you tons of sports physiology benefits, but fun is the bottom line in this activity.

COMMENTS:

This is a great short introduction drill that the youngest of the young love. The beauty of this drill, which is not really a drill but more of an activity, is that the parent or coach need not be concerned about technique. There are no style points in the bubble hit. A side note is that with young kids, I love those big red plastic bats with an oversized sweet spot.

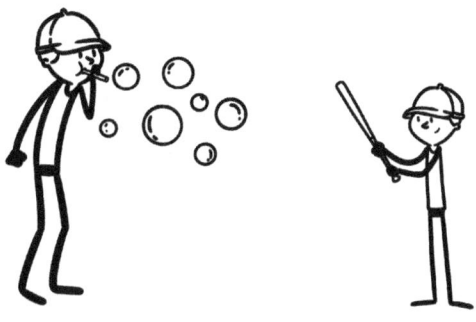

#14 Tee Ball Target Hit

THE SET-UP

You'll need a batting tee, a soft-covered baseball, and some animal stickers. Place the stickers on the baseball to create a focus point for the players. The batter is instructed to swing the bat and aim directly at the animal sticker.

WHO IS THIS DRILL GOOD FOR?

This is a great technique for first-time tee ball players. Just like the color code fielding drill with color baseballs, sometimes the simplest adjustment can make all the difference for success in young players who never hit the ball off the batting tee.

WHY IS IT BENEFICIAL?

This little technique helps motivate the young players to keep their eyes on the ball or sticker as they swing the bat. Teaching "eyes on the ball" in tee ball and youth baseball isn't just about better swings or catches — it's about building focus, confidence, coordination, and foundational athletic skills that transfer to all sports.

COMMENTS:

I have tried using fruit stickers and even coloring the baseballs, and found that the animal stickers worked best. And make sure you have duplicate stickers of the same animal. Some of the younger kids will yell things like, "I want to hit the elephant." Be flexible with this technique. Use stickers on bigger balls early in the season, and you should be able to use the stickers in regular tee ball games to help the batter succeed.

#15 Miss The Tee

THE SET-UP

This is a simple yet challenging drill for some. We need a batting tee, a plastic bat, or a broomstick with a string tied to the end so it hangs down. The tee ball players will also need a bat to swing. The coach or parent will hold the bat with the string hanging down over the batting tee. The batter is instructed to swing the bat so it doesn't hit the tee or the string.

WHO IS THIS DRILL GOOD FOR?

This is a good drill for all tee ball players. We are implementing "bat control" for young kids in a way that gives them an outstanding chance to succeed.

WHY IS IT BENEFICIAL?

In tee ball, "bat control" means a young player can hold, swing, and guide the bat with intention rather than just wildly swinging at the ball. While it might sound like an advanced skill, teaching bat control early on is critical to helping players build a solid foundation for future success in baseball and softball.

COMMENTS:

Bat control at the tee ball level is a challenge for many young players. The beauty of this drill is that the coach or parent controls the space between the string and the batting tee. Make the success rate almost impossible not to fail by making the space very wide for the players' first few swings. Slowly narrow the space, and if the batter hits either the tee or rope, widen the space. Always end this drill with a successful swing.

#16 Recycle Bin Tee Drill

THE SET-UP

Grab your recycling bin and remove any sharp or potentially hazardous items. Place only the safe items, one at a time, on the batting tee, and let the players hit them off. This makes for a great at-home drill.

WHO IS THIS DRILL GOOD FOR?

This drill works well for tee ball players of all ages, thanks to the creativity involved and the familiarity of the objects being hit.

WHY IS IT BENEFICIAL?

In tee ball, structure does matter — but flexibility and creativity are where real connection and learning happen. They create an environment where kids feel safe to try, fail, laugh, and grow. And even though structure is good, in tee ball, excessive rigidity can stifle development and extinguish a child's budding interest in sports. Flexibility and creativity can transform the season into a dynamic, engaging, and confidence-building journey. Kids may remember the creativity a coach or parent uses in practice or at home more than the games themselves.

COMMENTS:

Objects in the bin will vary in size. Start out using the bigger object, such as large detergent containers or milk gallon containers. To help stabilize and balance the larger items, use a short, clean bathroom plunger put into the tee. What makes this drill so popular with kids is that they all relate to the responsibility of recycling. I can't emphasize enough to make sure you take out all the dangerous, potentially injury-causing items from the bin.

#17 King Arthur

THE SET-UP

For this drill, use a broomstick or closet pole along with plastic balls like wiffle balls or pickle balls. The player grips the broomstick so the hands aren't spread too far apart, allowing better control. A coach or parent tosses the ball, and the player must make contact depending on which side of the stick the ball is headed.

WHO IS THIS DRILL GOOD FOR?

This drill may be a bit tougher for the youngest tee ball players. If you try this in practice, I'd do it toward the middle of the season as the players develop their confidence.

WHY IS IT BENEFICIAL?

Tee ball is the perfect age to develop hand-eye coordination. Even though tee ball primarily uses a stationary ball, drills that challenge hand-eye coordination are incredibly beneficial, laying a crucial foundation for future baseball success and overall athletic development. Including drills such as King Arthur that challenge this skill, players build lifelong athletic abilities that serve them across sports and in daily life.

COMMENTS:

Rag balls, clean rags rolled up with 1" and 2" masking tape on it, can also be used in this drill. This is a perfect at-home drill. When players get the knack of it, they love it. Keep in mind the broomstick is very thin, about 3/4-1 inch, and the closet pole measures 1 3/8 inches. It is a good idea to get the closet pole, giving players the best chance for success.

#18 Run Through The Base

THE SET-UP

Put a cone anywhere from five feet to fifteen feet beyond first base, but in line with the base. The players will line up at home plate and, one at a time, run to first base, touching it, and continue running to the cone. Once there, they turn toward foul territory and go to the end of the line.

WHO IS THIS DRILL GOOD FOR?

Teaching tee ball players the concept of "running through first base" is beneficial for every single player on the team, regardless of their current skill level. It's a fundamental baseball concept that serves multiple important purposes at the introductory level and builds crucial habits for future development. I encourage coaches to do this drill even after tee ball.

WHY IS IT BENEFICIAL?

This seemingly small detail carries significant benefits for these young athletes, setting them up for success and safety as they grow in the sport. When a runner stops abruptly on first base, they are slowing down, which is counter to the base running concept of running hard to beat the throw. Running through the base can determine if the runner will be safe or out.

COMMENTS:

Some things will drive coaches crazy. Stopping at first base instead of running hard is one of those things. This goes beyond tee ball. Practice this drill and practice it some more. Hopefully, the muscle memory will dominate! Remember what I said earlier: if you continue to coach baseball or softball, practice baserunning. Most coaches won't, and this is your chance to get a competitive edge.

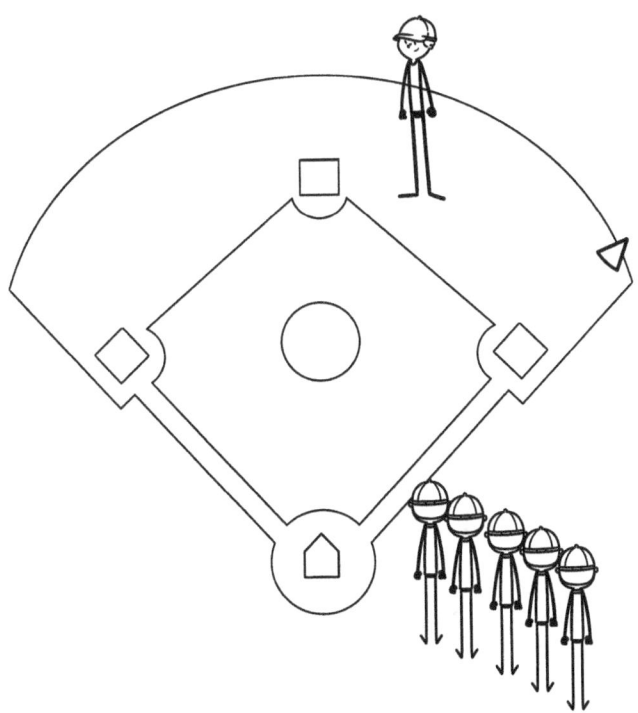

#19 Obstacle Course

THE SET-UP

Setting up an obstacle course for tee ball players is flexible and depends on space, number of kids, and skills you want to cover, with safety always the top priority. Recommended skills to include are: hitting off a tee, running to first, throwing a ball through a hoop, sliding into a base, catching a pop-up, tossing multiple balls into space, and finishing back at the start.

WHO IS THIS DRILL GOOD FOR?

The obstacle course is good for the whole team. But if there is ample room and enough assistant coaches, consider having two obstacle courses, with one being more challenging than the other.

WHY IS IT BENEFICIAL?

An obstacle course in tee ball does more than entertain—it builds skills, improves motor development, and keeps kids excited about learning the game. By mixing creativity with baseball fundamentals, coaches create an environment where players thrive physically and emotionally. Its benefits include incorporating multiple skills learned during the season into one fun activity.

COMMENTS:

I love obstacle courses! And I love them at all levels in all sports. In tee ball, I prefer to have the obstacle course toward the end of the year. The balls must be soft-covered for safety. And as much as I like no standing around, this is one activity that works smoother when only one player goes at a time.

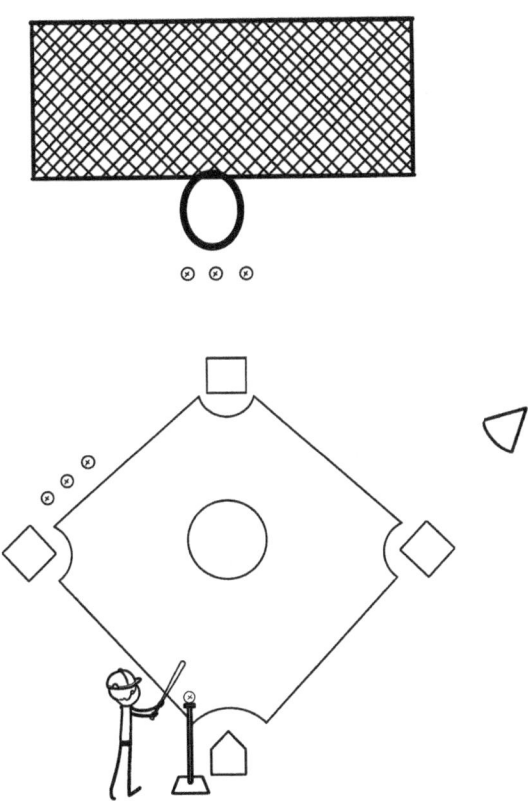

#20 Knock Down Fielding Drill

THE SET-UP

This is a one-on-one drill with the coach and the player. It is one of the best introductory drills you can do at home. All non-threatening items are used, such as multiple hackey sacks, bean bags, plastic golf balls, rag balls, and yarn balls. The player stands 6-10' away from the parent or coach without gloves. The parent throws the soft objects to the player, who moves his hand (try to use the glove hand) to make contact with the objects. The coach will throw them from side to side.

WHO IS THIS DRILL GOOD FOR?

This is not only good for all tee ball-aged kids, but pre-tee-ball age kids should try this.

WHY IS IT BENEFICIAL?

This drill builds the connection between what the eyes track and how the hands and body react, which is essential for fielding, hitting a moving ball, and catching later on. It's a softer form of reaction training, designed so young players learn in a safe way, knowing that with non-threatening items the chance of injury is very low. The goal is to get the player moving his glove hand around just as he would during real fielding.

COMMENTS:

In this drill, the player should aim to make contact with the object with fingers pointed up. The coach or parent alternates sides when tossing the object. To begin, the drill is stationary, but after some practice, the player can be asked to move a few steps in either direction.

#21 Hit The Water Spray Drill

THE SET-UP

Sometimes impulsively, if your creative juices are working, you can create a drill from another activity that has nothing to do with baseball. When I was outside with my kids in the summer, playing in the sprinkler, this drill was born. All you need is a running hose, a big red plastic bat, bathing suits, and laughter. With a running hose, the parent will direct the water intermittently, putting his thumb on the flow to control it. When the water comes to the player, he swings the bat at the strips of water coming at him.

WHO IS THIS DRILL GOOD FOR?

This drill is great for anyone who loves fun!

WHY IS IT BENEFICIAL?

It's a fantastic idea for tee ball kids and parents to "change it up" with different activities at home! This approach complements structured practice and provides numerous benefits for a child's overall development and their enjoyment of baseball. An activity like this creates a playful bridge between formal practice and a child's natural inclination to play, fostering skills, confidence, and a lifelong love for being active.

COMMENTS:

Make sure the players swinging the bat realize that the water coming to him intermittently means that he will have to take quick swings one right after the other. I've done this with my family and at end-of-year team pool parties.

Chapter 4

Beyond Tee Ball

Many of you reading this book will want to continue coaching and move on to baseball or softball at the next level. As a bonus, I've included 10 drills that go beyond tee ball. If you explore my other works — videos, books, and articles — you'll see I've shared well over 1,000 drills. But here's the truth: the best drills are always the ones your players actually love doing and ask for again. And sometimes, the very best drills are the ones you create yourself. Don't underestimate the creativity of your players, either. Once, during a drill I had designed, a player named Danny raised his hand and said:

"Coach, wouldn't this drill work better if we moved this line in and shifted that one toward second base?"

We tried his adjustment — and he was right. The drill flowed better, and the kids enjoyed it more. That moment stuck with me as a reminder: keep your coaching brain open and flexible. Great ideas can come from anywhere. Of course, baseball and softball practices can look very different depending on where you are. A practice in Des Moines, Iowa, will never look exactly like one in New York City. But the core principle remains the same no matter the setting: combine skill-building with fun so that players stay engaged, challenged, and excited to return. One area that becomes even more important as players grow older is warm-ups. A proper warm-up is not just a formality—it's essential for preventing injuries and maximizing performance. Light aerobic activity followed by dynamic stretching increases blood flow, improves joint mobility, and helps players mentally shift into practice mode. Research shows that structured warm-ups can reduce arm and leg injuries in youth athletes by as much as 36%. [3]

That's a number no coach should ignore.

Finally, remember this: practices are the true classroom for young athletes. Games may get the cheers and the headlines, but practices are where players learn, grow, and develop confidence. It's where mistakes can be corrected in a safe environment, and where you can reinforce habits that last a lifetime. A well-run practice teaches far more than hitting or fielding—it teaches resilience, teamwork, focus, and problem-solving. That's the real magic of coaching beyond tee ball.

#1 Third Base Drill

THE SET-UP

One of my staple drills is the *Third Base Drill*, which I use at nearly every practice. I split the team into three groups—one at third base, one at first, and one at home plate. I hit a ground ball to the first player at third, who fields it and throws to first. The first baseman then throws to home. After the play, each fielder rotates to the back of their line, with the catcher staying put. Once everyone has gone, the groups rotate clockwise: third moves to first, first to home, and home to third.

WHO IS THIS DRILL GOOD FOR?

This drill is good for players of all ages. Depending on the age group and the skills of the players, feel free to shorten or lengthen the throw.

WHY IS IT BENEFICIAL?

The throw from third base is the longest in the infield. We want players to be confident, almost overconfident, during a game, wanting the batter to hit the ball to me instead of the thought, "I hope he doesn't hit it to me."

COMMENTS:

At home plate, I keep the catcher in place to cut down on congestion and lower the risk of injury. To keep the pace up, I use two balls—after one is hit, the catcher underhands the next to me right away. Every so often, I mix in a "bobble drill" on a player's last rep. When they hear it, they field the ball, purposely bobble it by dropping it, then recover and throw to first. This reinforces that even after a mistake, they can still make the out.

#2 Rapid Throw Drill

THE SET-UP

A competitive favorite, this *Rapid-Fire Drill* teaches players to quickly transfer the ball from their glove to their throwing hand. Divide the team into pairs of similar skill, avoiding a combination of your two best or two weakest players. Each pair stands 25-35 feet apart, with one partner holding a ball. On your "Go" command, they will throw the ball back and forth as rapidly as possible for 15 seconds.

WHO IS THIS DRILL GOOD FOR?

This drill is good for players above 10 years old. You can try it with younger kids, but use soft-covered baseballs with them.

WHY IS IT BENEFICIAL?

This drill teaches ball transfer and the importance of controlling the ball, even though speed is part of the drill. You'll notice that once players do this drill a lot, their footwork almost auto-corrects itself with the right form, which helps with the speed.

COMMENTS:

Put a second ball at the feet of one player on each team in case there is an overthrow, they can go right to the second ball to still be in the drill. You can increase the time going from 15 seconds to 20 or more. After one or two turns, I like to move the players back five steps at a time. After each turn, go up and down the line asking how many throws they made. Players are on the honor system, and it works well. This is one of those drills where you have to space out the players next to each other very liberally.

#3 Outfield Relay Drill

THE SET-UP

The team is split in half, with one in left center and one in right center, each with a coach and a bucket of baseballs. At home plate, create a pyramid with 6 plastic buckets and a cone on top. One player from each team will be in the infield. One team goes first, and the coach throws the ball behind the first outfielder. On "go," the outfielder turns, locates the ball, runs to it and picks it up, throws to the infielder, who turns and tries to knock down the buckets.

WHO IS THIS DRILL GOOD FOR?

I have used this drill for kids as young as 8 and as old as 18. With the younger kids, you can shorten the field and even increase the number of buckets, making the task more achievable.

WHY IS IT BENEFICIAL?

Rarely do you create a fun game that teaches excellent concepts to your players, and the situation shows up in a game. *The Outfield Relay Drill* is one of those. We are teaching outfielders to hit the infielders while creating a target. We are teaching the infielder to turn to the glove side.

COMMENTS:

This drill is effective. The infielder waves his arms so the outfielder locks in and delivers the ball on a fly. If the ball is deeper, teach the infielder to move toward it, always turning to his glove side. Scoring works like this: hitting the infielder on a fly earns one point, turning glove side earns one point, and knocking down the buckets earns two points. After that, rotate players.

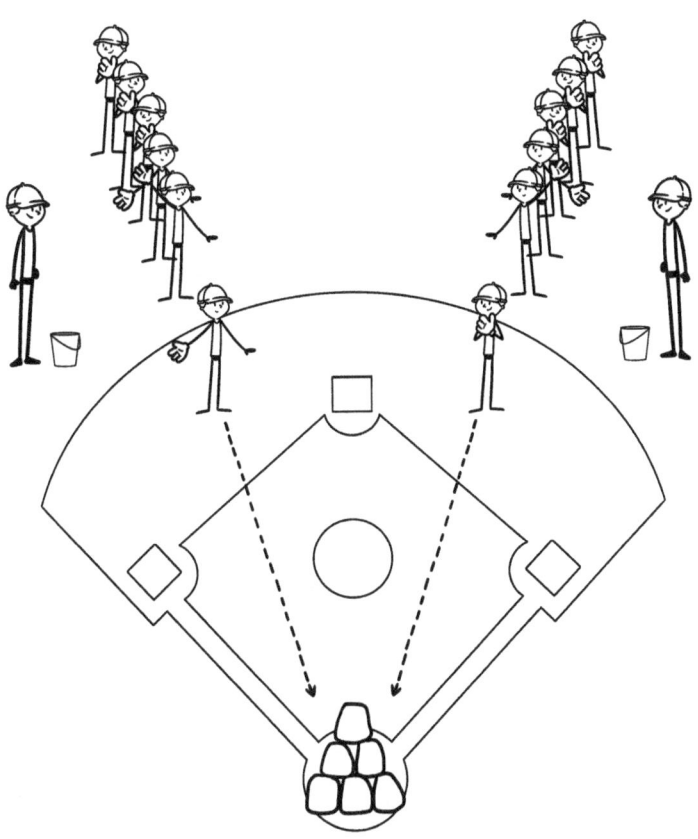

#4 Face-to-Face Drill

THE SET-UP

Form two lines facing each other. The first player in one line throws a baseball to the first player in the opposite line. After the throw, he can either move to the end of his own line or run down the side and join the end of the other line. The second option helps keep everyone moving. Because this drill uses a confined space, I recommend soft-covered balls for safety.

WHO IS THIS DRILL GOOD FOR?

When I was a young assistant coach helping another coach during All-Stars, we arrived to play a team in another league. We got there late, and there was no room to warm up anywhere, and we had very little time before our game was to start. Knowing the area was narrow and not wide, we quickly improvised, coming up with this drill.

WHY IS IT BENEFICIAL?

Though this drill may not make the annals of great creativity, I wanted to include it here in case you find yourself in the same situation, faced with very limited time and space to warm up.

COMMENTS:

This drill works well in limited space. I used to have players throw line drives, but given the confined area and the running to the other line, it's safest to stick with ground balls.

Make sure a coach is positioned in front of each line. For added safety, space the first player slightly in front of the line.

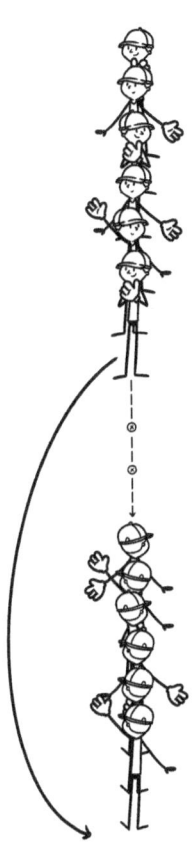

#5 Cross Infield Drill

THE SET-UP

This drill combines high reps with lots of movement —
my favorite kind. Set up four lines of players facing home
plate: two lines between 1st and 2nd, and two between 2nd
and 3rd. One coach stands in foul territory between home
and 3rd; another between home and 1st. Each coach has a
player next to them acting as a first baseman. The coach
between home and 3rd hits grounders to the lines between 1st
and 2nd; the coach between home and 1st hits to the other
lines.

WHO IS THIS DRILL GOOD FOR?

Those ten years old and above should get the concepts of
this drill. Some will have to grow into this drill and will get
better as the season goes on. Feel free to start with only one
line between the bases and grow to two lines as the players get
comfortable.

WHY IS IT BENEFICIAL?

Baseball drills with high reps and constant movement are
ideal because they build skills and keep players engaged.
Repetition develops muscle memory, improving consistency
under pressure. Movement boosts energy, limits downtime,
and helps maintain focus — especially for younger athletes.

COMMENTS:

First, note that the picture doesn't show the player near the coach acting as the first baseman—this is important. After a player takes their turn, they move to the end of the line next to them. A key safety point: if a coach mishits a ball and it dribbles out, the player must not charge it, as they risk being hit by a ball from the other line. On a mishit, the coach should immediately yell, "Leave it."

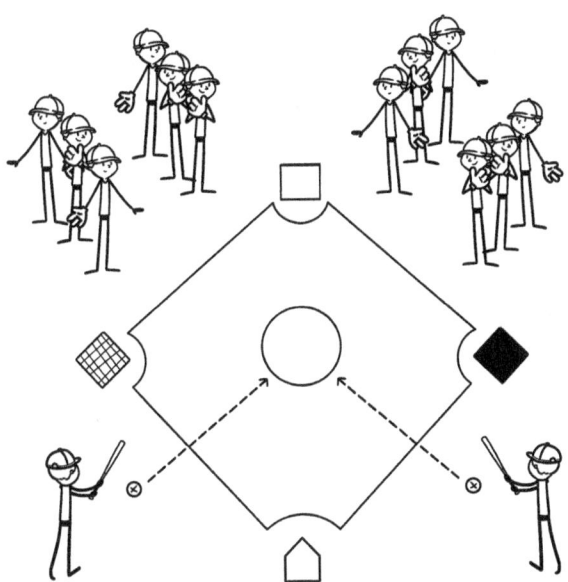

#6 Baserunning Sign Drill

THE SET-UP

This drill may seem basic, but it's essential. You'll need an infield with bases and three drop-down bases. Set them up to create two lines, keeping players spaced out. A coach in the third base box gives a sign to the first player in each line near first. A coach on the mound throws a pitch, and the baserunners react based on the sign.

WHO IS THIS DRILL GOOD FOR?

This drill is good for any team that already has signs from the coaches in action. We are trying to reinforce the signs while at the same time having players run between the bases efficiently.

WHY IS IT BENEFICIAL?

I always put a premium on base running. If you coach beyond tee ball, save time at each practice for baserunning. You'll get a leg up on the other coaches in your league.

COMMENTS:

I began emphasizing baserunning when I coached a team with limited talent and needed to find any edge I could. That edge turned out to be baserunning. In this drill, I use a few simple but effective signs: steal, fake steal, delayed steal, and a take-off-and-run sign. These add pressure on the defense and keep opponents guessing. I also noticed that when we regularly practiced baserunning, players on base became much more alert and aware of the game situation — they paid closer attention and made smarter decisions.

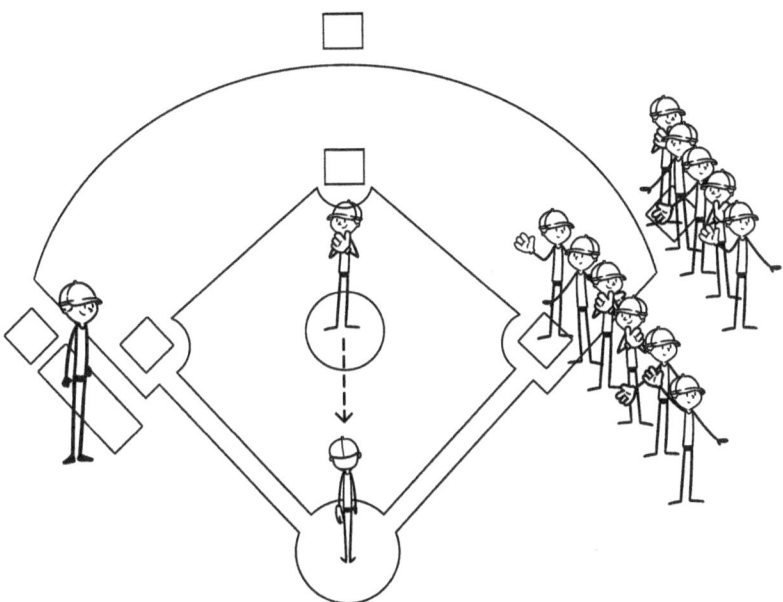

#7 Lead Drill

THE SET-UP

The players line up in a single file. The coach will have a bucket of balls next to him. The coach will line himself next to the first person in line. On the "go" command, the first player will run away from the coach and look over his shoulder as the coach throws a fly ball. The player catches the ball while on the move.

WHO IS THIS DRILL GOOD FOR?

You can do this drill with very young kids, even as young as 8 years old, but you may need to shorten the throwing distance. With younger players, use the "progression method": first, have them simply make contact with the glove, then gradually progress to catching the ball.

WHY IS IT BENEFICIAL?

Practicing catching a fly ball on the move is valuable because it closely mirrors real game situations. Most plays require tracking the ball while running at different angles and speeds. It is difficult for first-time players to run and catch the ball. Though this drill has players running in a straight line, it is a great introduction to catching the ball on the move.

COMMENTS:

Start with soft-covered balls, then progress to harder ones. Position players so they run toward the sun, ensuring that when they turn back to track the ball, the glare is behind them. If space allows and you have assistant coaches, run two lines simultaneously, with one line starting where the other finishes. Safety is key. For a backyard version, parents can place multiple balls in a glove. As the child catches a ball on the run, they simply remove it, roll it on the ground, and continue running to catch the next one.

#8 Rag Ball Home Run Derby

THE SET-UP

For this fun game, all you really need is a cement or brick wall, chalk, rag balls, and a bat. If you don't have a wall, you can do what I did in my backyard. I set up a tarp using 4 bicycle hooks in two trees, one high and one low. Then I got four bungee cords and wrapped them around two trees, one high and one low. Stick the end into the four corners of a blue tarp that has rings with holes in them. With duct tape, I make two squares, one inside the other. If using a wall, do the same with chalk. Whether doing the toss drill or hitting off the batting tee, a ball that lands inside the big square counts as a single, inside the small square is a home run, and anything else is an out.

WHO IS THIS DRILL GOOD FOR?

This drill works well for kids of any age. It's perfect for at-home practice or, if at a schoolyard, set it up against a wall with two or more teams. The game moves quickly and is a ton of fun.

WHY IS IT BENEFICIAL?

This drill is a ton of fun, and it really gets the kids focusing on precision as they aim for the small box to score a home run.

COMMENTS:

Rag balls are simply clean rags wrapped with one- or two-inch masking tape. While wiffle balls and pickle balls work well with a tarp, they can ricochet unpredictably off a wall, so stick with rag balls. Don't wrap them too tightly, or they'll bounce back too hard. If you're making a tarp setup, involve the kids in constructing it—it's part of the fun. For a visual guide, check out my free video *Backyard Baseball Drills* on the Schupak Sports YouTube channel. This is 100% pure fun!

#9 Home Run Derby

THE SET-UP
This fun game gives players a chance to hit one over the fence. Take 2 drop-down bases and place them between the pitcher's mound in a straight line. The 3 bases will simulate home plate. Second base is for 10 year-olds, the drop down base in the middle for 11 year-olds, and other drop-down base for 12 year-olds.

WHO IS THIS DRILL GOOD FOR?
This fun game has been one of my top 3 fun drills to end practice. All players love it. When you see a small framed 10 year-old hit one over the fence, you'll love the reaction.

WHY IS IT BENEFICIAL?
Ending practice with a game like *Home Run Derby* helps the team associate baseball with enjoyment. Psychologically, finishing with success or laughter boosts confidence and motivation, making players more receptive to learning and more likely to stay committed throughout the season. This positive closure is especially valuable for keeping 10–12 year-olds enthusiastic and building a lifelong love of the game. What kid doesn't like to hit a home run?

COMMENTS:
When I was very young, we had Home Run Derby featuring names like Aaron, Banks, Killebrew, Mantle, and Mays. Though it lasted only a short time, the game resonated

with me and was one of the most exciting competitions I ever saw. Renewed in 1985, the Derby has become a staple of All-Star week. Kids love it — and it's the perfect use for those old waterlogged baseballs.

#10 Efficient Batting Practice

THE SET-UP

All players get numbers as they arrive at practice. Number 1 bats first, etc. Four cones are set up near home as bunting targets. The batter gets a predetermined number of swings. They must bunt the first two pitches. If the bunts go through the cones, they get 2 extra swings. The on-deck batter is ready to hit, sitting in the dugout. The double on-deck batter is on the other side of the fence, hitting off the batting tee. If there is enough room and coaches, a triple on-deck batter is doing the toss drill outside the fence.

WHO IS THIS DRILL GOOD FOR?

This is good for any team that ends practice with batting practice.

WHY IS IT BENEFICIAL?

Efficient batting practice is essential because it maximizes the number of quality swings each player gets while keeping the pace fast and engaging. Well-organized sessions prevent long waits, maintain focus, and allow coaches to address mechanics in real time. Kids live for batting practice. Don't deny it, make it fun.

COMMENTS:

When players arrive on time to practice, they get more quality swings and improve bunting across the team. This method works—and works well. Adjust or modify it to ensure every player gets the most out of the one thing they all love about baseball: batting! For a more detailed description, see my book *Baseball Coaching: A Guide for the Youth Coach and Parent*, available for free at your local library.

54 Tee Ball Tips

1. Communicate with the team as soon as the roster is picked.

2. Have a Parents' Meeting early in the season.

3. Coaches should make a concerted effort to learn every player's name as soon as possible.

4. The primary goal of tee ball is to build a love for the game.

5. Early practices, separate skills. If teaching throwing, don't have players catch. If teaching catching, no throwing.

6. Kids learn at different speeds. Be patient with every player, especially with their struggles.

7. Focus on praising effort and good behavior, not just results.

8. Expose kids to skills in a positive manner and don't be intent on having them master each one.

9. Mix in non-baseball games like "Red Light, Green Light" to keep kids engaged.

10. Your attitude as a parent or coach is infectious. Keep it positive.

11. Encourage kids to cheer for their teammates, whether in the field or at the plate.

12. Let kids know it's okay to make mistakes: it's how they learn.

13. Produce a team newsletter, a hard copy. Print it three times during the season. Mention every team member. Print extra copies. Remember the grandparents.

14. Start and end practices on time.

15. Have a written plan for each practice.

16. Start each practice with a 5-10 minute warm-up.

17. Minimize standing in lines — keep kids moving. Break into small groups to increase repetitions.

18. Practices should be between 45 and 60 minutes. Anything longer and you'll probably lose their focus.

19. Utilize assistant coaches and parents at practice.

20. Rotate stations to keep practice fresh.

21. Use short, high-energy drills.

22. Always have a backup drill in case one flops.

23. Use visual aids like cones to teach field positioning (left, center, right field).

24. Keep pep talks short and do them at a different base at the start of each practice.

25. Never let a player leave an at-bat without hitting a ball off the tee. Increase the size of the ball or anything else.

26. Include warm-up and cool-down routines.

27. Review safety rules before starting drills.

28. Give all players equal playing time.

29. Rotate positions so kids learn the whole field.

30. Rotate the batting order every inning.

31. Praise hustle even if the play fails.

32. Deviate from the rule book if necessary, so players will be in a position to succeed.

33. Keep parents informed about rules and expectations.

34. Maintain a positive, encouraging dugout atmosphere.

35. Everyone must help clean the dugout before leaving the field.

36. Ask parents to cheer for effort, not just hits.

37. Share practice tips with parents so kids can work at home.

38. Be aware that there are a variety of situations and economic differences with each family.

39. Invite parents to team-bonding events.

40. An end-of-year team party and a parent/player tee ball game is a great activity.

41. Recognize parent volunteers publicly.

42. Remind parents that every kid develops at their own pace.

43. Always finish practice with a fun game or a cheer to leave a positive impression.

44. Encourage kids to have their own water bottle with their name on it, but always have a team water jug with plenty of cups.

45. Always have a black Sharpie pen if players' items are not tagged with their names.

46. Early in the season, make sure parents know it can get cool during the game.

47. Keep an open line of communication with parents and coaches to address any concerns.

48. Coaches should be proactive if they sense a parent is unhappy about something.

49. Once or twice a year, have a cell phone-free game so no one has a phone in the stands or dugout.

50. Embrace the unpredictable nature of tee ball like running to the wrong base.

51. If a grandparent is watching from each team, have a very short ceremonial first pitch for each team.

52. Shift the spotlight from "looking right" to "trying hard," making success easier and more rewarding.

53. This time goes by fast. Treasure every moment you have on the field.

54. Keep it fun and positive!

Chapter 5

Closing

Sports have been a huge part of my life, perhaps too much at times, but I learned long ago that you cannot live wearing another man's shoes. You take what stirs your blood, you hold to what you love, and you make peace with the rest. For me, that passion has always been sports. In writing *Tee Ball Myths & Solutions*, I wanted to give you more than drills or practice plans. I hoped to offer ideas, yes, but also a way of seeing — to invite you to think, to imagine, to shape your own path as a coach and as a parent. The goal was never perfection. It was creativity, connection, and the kind of joy that comes when a child's laughter meets the crack of a bat — or the smile that breaks across a face when a ball finally rolls fair off the tee.

This journey is not an ending but a beginning. Some of what I've shared may help you on the field, some at the dinner table, and perhaps — if I've succeeded — even in those small, quiet moments that make up family life. Time with your children is the one treasure that only diminishes if ignored and grows brighter when embraced. It is the measure of days that will not come again.

I often think of a story about a father and son that lingers in my mind. Mike Chernoff, General Manager of the Cleveland Guardians, and his father, Mark, a longtime New York radio executive, began a tradition when Mike was six years-old. Having a catch. And the tradition continued. Once a month, no matter how full their calendars, they meet halfway between New York and Cleveland, in a place called Snow Shoe, Pennsylvania, to play catch. Two men, bound by a ball tossed back and forth across years, across distance, across the noise of the world. There is beauty in its simplicity. What could be more ordinary? And what could matter more? Those are the stories I love most to tell. They remind me, and I hope they remind you, that the true game is not only on the field but between people, in the bonds we make and tend to over time. And then there's tee ball. A bat, a tee, a ball that sometimes dribbles three feet — but hidden inside is a chance to build a memory that will outlast box scores and trophies. It is the smallest field, yet it holds the largest promise.

I'll leave you with a quote from former pitcher and writer Jim Bouton:

"You spend a good piece of your life gripping a baseball, and in the end it turns out that it was the other way around all the time."

Marty Schupak's Coaching Resources

I have worked to make all my products available for free. The first place I'd look for content is my YouTube channel, which you can reach at: www.SchupakSports.com

Most of my videos are free on YouTube and also available at your local library through three programs: Hoopla, Kanopy, and Overdrive.

For my books, many are available as e-books at your local library. If they don't have them, request them — they will usually order them for you. If you have trouble locating any of my products, contact me directly at: **greenrewind@gmail.com**

Baseball Videos
T–Ball Skills & Drills
The 59 Minute Baseball Practice
Backyard Baseball Drills
Winning Baseball Strategies
Pitching Drills & Techniques
Hitting Drills & Techniques
Baserunning & Bunting Drills
Drills & Techniques For The Catcher
Fielding Drills & Techniques
Infield Team Play & Strategies
44 Baseball Mistakes & Corrections
Advanced Toss And Batting Tee Drills

Baseball Books
Championship Baseball Drills
T-Ball Drills
T-Ball Skills & Drills
44 Baseball Mistakes & Corrections
Baseball Coaching: A Guide For The Youth Coach & Parent
Baseball Chronicles: Articles On Youth Baseball
Baseball Chronicles 2: Articles On Youth Baseball

Playoff Fever & Split Pants (from the Cliff Vermont series)
Shoot The Pill & Smashed Puzzle (from the Cliff Vermont series)
Youth Baseball Drills

Basketball Videos
48 Championship Basketball Drills
Driveway Basketball Drills
Offensive Basketball Moves
Basketball Fundamentals

Basketball Books
Basketball Fundamentals
Basketball Chronicles: Articles On Youth Coaching

Other Sports Products By Marty Schupak
Championship Soccer Drills
Backyard Soccer Drills
34 Soccer Goalie Drills
Soccer Shooting Drills
Soccer Fast Footwork Drills
Advanced Soccer Drills
Backyard Golf
Championship Hockey Drills
Backyard Lacrosse
Backyard Sports
59 Minute Mem-Cards

I am a huge NFL fan who lives and dies with my New York Jets. If you are an NFL fan, check out my Podcast on all platforms, including Spotify, iTunes, and Apple Podcasts.

Keyword: Jets Rewind

End Notes

#1 -Robert P. Pangrazi and Aaron Beighle, Dynamic Physical Education for Elementary School Children, 19th ed., revised edition (Champaign, IL: Human Kinetics, 2020).

#2-Robert P. Pangrazi and Aaron Beighle, Dynamic Physical Education for Elementary School Children, 19th ed., revised edition (Champaign, IL: Human Kinetics, 2020).

#3-Ding L, Luo J, Smith D, Mackey M, Fu H, Davis M, Yanping H. Effectiveness of Warm-Up Intervention Programs to Prevent Sports Injuries among Children and Adolescents: A Systematic Review and Meta-Analysis. International Journal of Environmental Research and Public Health. 2022;19(10):6336–6353. This meta-analysis of 15 trials involving over 21,500 participants found a pooled injury rate ratio of ~0.64—indicating a 36% reduction in sports-related injuries with neuromuscular warm-up programs in youth athletes

Glossary

Athletic late bloomer: refers to an individual— often a child or adolescent — who develops their athletic abilities, physical skills, or sports performance later than their peers. While early bloomers may quickly show natural talent or excel in physical activities at a young age, late bloomers may take more time to develop coordination, strength, speed, or sport-specific skills but eventually catch up or even surpass others with continued practice, growth, and training.

Cognitive Growth: refers to the development of a child's thinking, reasoning, problem-solving, and information-processing abilities. In the context of sports, particularly tee ball, understanding cognitive development is paramount because it dictates what children are capable of understanding and how they learn. Tee ball is a foundational experience where children begin to integrate their developing cognitive abilities with physical movement and social interaction in a structured environment. Coaches who are aware of these cognitive stages are far more effective in creating a positive and truly developmental experience.

Coordination: is the ability to use different parts of the body together smoothly and efficiently, and it plays a central role in how kids learn and perform in sports from tee ball through high school athletics. As kids grow, their coordination develops in stages and is influenced by physical growth, nervous system development, and experience.

Growth plates: Areas of cartilage located near the ends of a child's long bones (e.g., in the wrists, elbows, knees, ankles). This is where new bone tissue forms, making the bones grow longer. They are weaker than surrounding ligaments and tendons, making them vulnerable to injury during rapid growth (growth spurts) from repetitive stress or impact. Common "growing pains" in athletes are often related to growth plate irritation (apophysitis).

Growth spurts: In children occur at various stages throughout childhood and adolescence, involving rapid increases in height, weight, and physical development. These stages can significantly impact their sports participation, especially in skill development, coordination, and physical readiness. Growth isn't linear; it happens in stages, and each stage affects how kids move, play, and respond to physical activity.

Motor Skills: refer to the physical abilities and movements involving the coordinated use of muscles to perform specific tasks essential to playing the sport. These include both gross motor skills, which use large muscle groups for actions like running, throwing, and swinging, and fine motor skills, which involve smaller muscle groups for precise movements like gripping the bat correctly or fielding the ball.

Muscle Memory: a neurological process where the brain and nervous system learn and retain specific motor skills through repeated practice, allowing players to perform movements automatically and with less conscious effort over time. In tee ball means the player's brain and body learn to perform baseball skills nearly automatically through repeated practice, improving consistency and enjoyment while reducing frustration.

Natural Athletic Ability: refers to the innate physical traits and talents a person possesses that may give them an advantage in sports, including attributes like speed, strength, agility, coordination, and endurance. In youth sports such as tee ball, natural athletic ability might show as a child who is naturally quick to react, has good hand-eye coordination, or displays agility and balance with ease. However, it is important to clarify that while some children may have natural talent, athletic ability is also heavily influenced by environment, practice, and training. Many experts emphasize that what appears as "natural athleticism" is often the result of early physical activity, learning motor skills, and repeated practice.

Overuse Injuries: Injuries that occur gradually over time from repetitive stress on muscles, tendons, bones, and joints without enough time for the body to recover. Examples include "Little League Elbow," Osgood-Schlatter disease (knee pain), and stress fractures.

Sports Overachiever: refers to an athlete—often a youth or amateur player—who performs at a level significantly beyond what might be expected based on their natural physical abilities, size, or early skill indicators. Overachievers tend to succeed through extraordinary dedication, hard work, mental toughness, and a strong commitment to training and improvement, rather than relying largely on innate talent or athleticism.

Sports specialization: In the context of youth sports, refers to the intense and often year-round training and competition in a single sport, often to the exclusion of other sports or physical activities. It essentially means a young athlete commits significant time, energy, and resources to one sport with the aim of achieving high levels of performance, potentially leading to elite status, college scholarships, or professional careers. While some rare exceptions (like gymnasts or figure skaters, where peak performance occurs at a younger age and highly complex skills need to be mastered before puberty) might benefit from earlier focused training, the overwhelming consensus among medical, coaching, and athletic development professionals strongly advises against early sports specialization for the vast majority of sports.

Sportsmanship: in youth sports is essentially about playing fair and treating everyone involved with respect, regardless of the outcome of the game. It goes beyond just following the rules; it encompasses the spirit of the game and a set of positive behaviors that build character and make the experience enjoyable for everyone.

About The Author

Marty Schupak coached youth sports for 30 years. He has coached and taught over 10,000 players, either on his teams or at his clinics. Many of these players have gone on to play in high school and beyond and some have received athletic scholarships to college. Thousands of youth coaches have also been trained at his clinics. He is the creator of 28 sports instructional videos including: T–Ball Skills & Drills, The 59 Minute Baseball Practice, Backyard Baseball Drills, Winning Baseball Strategies and Hitting Drills and Techniques. He has authored numerous books on baseball including the best selling Baseball Coaching: A Guide For The Youth Coach and Parent. He also authored the popular basketball book: Basketball Fundamentals.

He received a bachelor's degree from Boston University and a master's degree in physical education from Arizona State University. He is a nationally known speaker and has appeared on numerous radio shows, podcasts, and panel discussions. In his spare time, Marty collects sports memorabilia and follows his beloved New York Jets, as he has done since 1964. Marty lives in Valley Cottage, New York with his wife, Elaine.

www.ingramcontent.com/pod-product-compliance
Lightning Source LLC
Chambersburg PA
CBHW080902120626
46555CB00008B/2922